To M

P9-DBL-685

Praise for
You Can Be Happy No Matter What

"You will find Dr. Carlson's new approach very helpful — solid, sensible, and filled with loving guidance."

— Dr. Wayne Dyer,
author of *Your Erroneous Zones*

"*You Can Be Happy No Matter What* will appeal to those caught in the tangles of outmoded thinking. It speaks simply to us in a way that's most fitting when we want to move out of dysfunctions into robust, effective living."

— Marsha Sinetar,
author of *Developing a 21st-Century Mind*

"A profoundly simple, hopeful, and human book about what's available to us all — happiness."

— Joseph Bailey,
author of *The Serenity Principle*

From Neal
Enjoy!

YOU CAN BE
HAPPY
no matter what

Also by Richard Carlson, PhD

The *Don't Sweat the Small Stuff* Series

Don't Worry, Make Money

Easier Than You Think

For the Love of God (with Benjamin Shield, PhD)

Handbook for the Heart (with Benjamin Shield, PhD)

Handbook for the Soul (with Benjamin Shield, PhD)

Shortcut Through Therapy

Slowing Down to the Speed of Life (with Joseph Bailey)

Stop Thinking and Start Living

What About the Big Stuff?

You Can Feel Good Again

YOU CAN BE
HAPPY
no matter what

Five Principles for
Keeping Life in Perspective

15th Anniversary Edition

Richard Carlson, PhD

New World Library
Novato, California

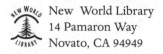 New World Library
14 Pamaron Way
Novato, CA 94949

Preface Copyright © 2006 by Richard Carlson, PhD
Revised edition Copyright © 1997 by Richard Carlson, PhD
Original edition Copyright © 1992 by Richard Carlson, PhD

Cover design: Tracy Cunningham
Text layout and design: Tona Pearce Myers

Library of Congress Cataloging-in-Publication Data
Carlson, Richard, 1961 May 16–
You can be happy no matter what : five principles for keeping life in perspective / Richard Carlson . -- 15th anniversary ed.
    p.   cm.
ISBN-13: 978-1-57731-568-1 (pbk. : alk. paper)
1. Happiness. 2. Contentment.   I. Title.
BF575.H27 C375 2006
97-15902
158.1—dc22   2006033782

First printing of this edition, January 2007
ISBN 978-1-57731-568-1
Printed in Canada

g New World Library is a proud member of the Green Press Initiative.

20   19   18   17   16

To my beautiful children —
may you always be happy
no matter what.

CONTENTS

Part One — The Principles

Part Two — Applying the Principles

PREFACE
to the 15th Anniversary Edition

TIME REALLY DOES SEEM TO FLY! It's been fifteen years since New World Library published the original edition of *You Can Be Happy No Matter What*. Around that time, my wife, Kris, and I had one two-year-old, Jazzy, and Kris was pregnant with our second daughter, Kenna. Today, the girls are teenagers, and the older one is preparing to leave for college. All of us — you, me, and everyone else — have gotten older. Our families, relationships, careers, and lives have changed dramatically — physically, financially, spiritually.

Recently, someone suggested to me that what I wrote in this book fifteen years ago was perfect for its time. But he felt very strongly that we now live in a completely different world — a more dangerous and less certain world than ever before. "It's far more difficult today to be happy than it was back in the nineties," he said.

While I certainly would agree that the world has changed a great deal, particularly since September 11, 2001, I'm happy to report that our capacity for happiness is the same as it has always been. Being happy is an inside job. As Wayne Dyer says in the foreword to this book, "Many people mistakenly believe that circumstances make a person. They don't. Instead, they reveal him or her." That statement was true fifteen years ago, it's true today, and it will be true fifteen years from now. We've always been able to point to certain people who face extremely difficult circumstances yet live extraordinary, happy lives. Conversely, of course, we can find plenty of people who enjoy wonderful circumstances full of every conceivable blessing yet live lives of perpetual unhappiness, even misery.

While circumstances do indeed change, both individually and collectively, what don't change are the universal principles that, when truly practiced, point us in the direction of happiness.

When our minds are still and quiet, one of the first things we discover is that our natural state is one of inner peace. This contented state of mind is always present whenever we are not interfering with it, not using our thinking as a weapon against ourselves. And when we experience this peaceful state of mind, it allows us to be happy, despite our imperfect circumstances and the chaotic world. What's more, when we learn to be happy and we have what we need emotionally, we are better equipped to make a positive difference in the world. In other words, we can't give what we don't have; if we're not happy, we can't contribute to the happiness of others.

This book explains five extraordinarily simple yet profound principles that, once understood and practiced, pave the way to a more content, peaceful, and happy life. All five principles explain how our minds operate and can, depending on how we use them, determine our level of well-being. Of course, no one is happy all the time, and you won't be after reading this book. You can, however, learn to get yourself back on track much more quickly than before. You can learn to avoid the type of thinking that will exacerbate any unhappiness you may be experiencing.

One thing has become extremely clear to me over the past fifteen years: Life is a gift to be treasured. When we remove the obstacles that originate in our own thinking, we begin to appreciate this gift like never before. My deepest hope is that everyone who reads this book will be positively touched in some way. If there's one thought I'd love to leave you with, it's this: You can be happy no matter what. You really can!

FOREWORD

MANY PEOPLE MISTAKENLY BELIEVE that circumstances make a person. They don't. Instead, they reveal him or her. Our circumstances don't define us; they represent our unique curriculum — our tests, challenges, and opportunities for personal growth, acceptance, and detachment. Our success as a human being does not lie in our collections of possessions or accomplishments. It does not lie in the details of our predicament, but in how we deal with what we have and how we face our challenges, how we transform our unique curriculum into growth and into a life filled with love.

We have the capacity to manifest our own destiny, to create "Real Magic" in our lives, to make our lives an expression of divinity, to remove ego from our consciousness, and to make love our top priority. To do these things, however, it's essential that we create an inner balance, a sense of harmony and equanimity within. Happiness is not the end of the road; it's the beginning. Contentment enhances our spiritual life.

The principles in this book act as navigational tools to help you find contentment in your life. They are like a set of operating instructions to guide you inward, where peace resides. They can help you remain centered and calm. As you become happier, you enter a new dimension of life that plants seeds for further spiritual growth. Without the constant struggle and distraction of stress, anger, conditions, and desires, your life will unfold with greater harmony.

In this extraordinary book, Dr. Carlson explains that life is not your enemy, but your thinking can be. He reminds us that our minds are very powerful tools that can work for us or against us at any given moment. We have a choice. We can learn to flow with life, with loving and patient acceptance, or we can struggle against it. I have said many times that we are spiritual beings having a human experience. We have the capacity to make this human experience all it can be. We have, within us, the resources to live a happy, fulfilled life regardless of the challenges we face. Read this book and reflect on its message. You will see that, despite outer experiences, it's true: You can be happy no matter what! God bless you.

— Dr. Wayne Dyer

ACKNOWLEDGMENTS

I WOULD LIKE TO ACKNOWLEDGE the following people: Patti Breitman for being happy enough to see what I was trying to say even before I finished saying it; Kristine Carlson for her loving encouragement; Sheila Krystal for being such a wonderful partner and friend; Carol LaRusso for such a lovely job editing and for taking the time to learn this approach; George and Linda Pransky for being wonderful teachers; and Barbara and Don Carlson for learning the beautiful gift of happiness — and sharing it with others.

YOU CAN BE
HAPPY
no matter what

INTRODUCTION

Happiness! It's something that all of us want but that few of us ever achieve. It is characterized by feelings of gratitude, inner peace, satisfaction, and affection for ourselves and for others. Our most natural state of mind is one of contentment and joy. The barriers or obstructions that keep us from experiencing these positive feelings are learned negative processes that we have innocently come to accept as "necessary," or as "just the way life is." When we uncover these inherent positive feelings and remove the obstructions keeping us from them, the result is a more meaningful and beautiful experience of life.

These positive feelings are not fleeting emotions that

come and go with changing circumstances, but permeate our lives and become part of us. Finding this state of mind allows us to be more lighthearted and easygoing, whether or not our circumstances seem to warrant this positive outlook. In this nicer state, life seems less complicated and our problems are lessened. The reason: When we feel better, we have more access to our own wisdom and common sense. We tend to be less reactive, defensive, and critical; we make better decisions and we communicate more effectively.

The best way to uncover these deep positive feelings within yourself is to begin to understand their source. There are five principles of psychological functioning that act as guides, or navigators, and will help you regain your natural sense of serenity. I call this natural state "healthy psychological functioning," or simply "a nice feeling." You will learn to detect and protect yourself from the psychological obstructions that have kept you from these positive feelings — those insecure thoughts that you have learned to take too seriously.

The first four principles of this book are based on a series of psychological principles that were originally formulated by Dr. Rick Suarez and Dr. Roger C. Mills.[*] They show you how to obtain access to this feeling of happiness whenever you like. Once understood, these principles allow you to feel happy and contented regardless of your problems — really! As a consultant who teaches these principles in my

---

[*] Rick Suarez, Roger C. Mills, and Darlene Stewart, *Sanity, Insanity, and Common Sense: The Groundbreaking New Approach to Happiness* (New York: Fawcett, Columbine, 1987).

own practice, I continually see people transform their lives in a more positive direction in spite of the difficult challenges they face. When you feel genuinely contented with your life, you will be able to solve any problem more easily and efficiently than you ever thought possible. The five principles I am about to introduce represent a profound breakthrough in the understanding of our human psychological functioning. They are remarkably simple, yet powerful, principles that explain how the mind works, and they can be used by all human beings regardless of where they live — they cross all cultural barriers. The principles are described in detail beginning in chapter 1, but I'll briefly summarize them here:

Thinking. Our ability to think creates our psychological experience of life, and thinking is a voluntary function.

Moods. Our own understanding that thinking is a voluntary function fluctuates from moment to moment and from day to day; these variances are called moods.

Separate Psychological Realities. Because we all think in a unique way, each of us lives in a separate psychological reality.

Feelings. Our feelings and emotions serve as a built-in biofeedback mechanism that lets us know how we are doing from a psychological standpoint.

The Present Moment. Learning to keep our attention in the present moment, by paying attention to our feelings, allows us to live at peak efficiency and without the distraction of negative thinking. The present moment is where we find happiness and inner peace.

Learning how your mind operates and functions allows you access to happiness — a magnificent feeling — which enables you to freely enjoy your life and your relationships. Most approaches to happiness advocate doing or changing something in your life. But experience shows us this is a temporary cure at best. The mind-set that tells us that to be happy, we must do something differently doesn't go away when the change has taken place. It then starts all over again looking for flaws and conditions that must be met and corrected before we can feel happy. When you understand the five principles of healthy psychological functioning, you can reverse this dynamic and feel happy right *now*, even if you and your life aren't perfect! Once you are feeling content, and no longer distracted by your false negativity, better access to your true wisdom and common sense will allow you to see solutions and alternatives that had been buried under weighty concerns and busy internal dialogue.

Contentment is the foundation to a fulfilling life. It brings with it good relationships, job satisfaction, parenting skills (for those of us who are parents), and the wisdom and common sense it takes to move through life in a graceful manner. Without contentment, life can seem like a battle-ground where we are too busy struggling with problems to enjoy life's beauty. Consumed by concerns, hoping that someday things will be better, we postpone satisfaction while life slips away. With a happy feeling, we can enjoy life fully — right now. Obviously, your problems are very "real" and significant, but once you learn how to be contented, problems won't stop you from enjoying your life. A con-tented feeling brings with it childlike enjoyment — a light-hearted way of being in the world that opens a channel of appreciation for simple things, to feel grateful for the mag-nificent gift of life itself.

This new understanding can be applied to all of life's challenges. You'll learn no sophisticated techniques or "cop-ing mechanisms" to deal with each specific problem; you will just learn to live in a more contented state of mind: a state of love. The beautiful part of this knowledge — once you understand healthy psychological functioning — is that this knowledge lasts. It's not that you'll never again lose hold of the feeling of love — you will — but when you do, you'll understand how you got off-course, and know exactly how to point yourself back in a better direction.

The Key to Happiness: Your Mind

Your mind essentially serves you in two ways. It is a storage vault for information and past experience, and is also a transmitter for wisdom and common sense. The storage vault, or "computer," part of your brain is used to analyze, compare, relate facts, and make computations. The value of this component is clear: without it, we couldn't survive. The other part of the brain, the "transmitter" that we each have access to, is the part that deals with matters of the heart — where computer information is insufficient. It is our transmitter mind, not our computer mind, that is the source of our contentment, joy, and wisdom.

Part of the process of obtaining access to this other part of ourselves is to recognize how necessary and practical it is. How inappropriate it would be to use a computer to solve a marriage or career problem, or to decide how to talk to your teenager about drugs or to your toddler about discipline. Most people wouldn't use a computer for these personal, heartfelt problems; they require softness and wisdom. Unless we understand and value the "transmitter" part of ourselves (healthy psychological functioning), we have no alternative but to call on the "computer" to deal with our personal issues. New answers don't come from what you already know in the computer part of your brain. *They come from a change of heart, from seeing life differently, from the unknown, quieter part of yourself.*

Let's illustrate this point with the familiar story of someone who has lost his keys. He thinks and thinks (computer thinking) about where they could be, but to no avail. He simply can't remember. Then, just when he has given up thinking to gaze out the window instead, the answer suddenly pops into his head and he remembers exactly where he left them. The answer came when he cleared his head, and not from the excessive thinking which would not allow

the answer to surface. All of us have had similar experiences, but few have learned the valuable lesson of "not
knowing" in order to know. Instead, we continue to think
that the answer comes from racking our brains, from using
our "computer."

You can learn to access and trust this healthy psychological functioning — the quiet part of your mind that is
the source of inherent positive feelings, the wise part of
you that knows the answers. And when it doesn't know, it
knows that it doesn't. You can learn the difference between
computer thinking and creative thinking — when to trust
your computer, and when it's appropriate to back off and
quiet down.

The goal of this book is to help you experience this
nicer state of mind (contentment) more often in your life.
When people learn to live in this peaceful state of mind,
they discover that happiness and contentment are, in fact,
independent from their circumstances. It's not that things
shouldn't go "right," — of course that's best — but things don't
always have to go right *before* we can be happy. We don't always have power over other people and/or events, but we
do have tremendous power to feel happy and contented
with our life. One nice by-product of feeling happy "for no
reason" is that troubling details begin to work themselves
out. We actually think better, more clearly, and more intel-
ligently when our minds are not full of boggling concerns.

Our minds can work for us or against us at any given
moment. We can learn to accept and live with the natural
psychological laws that govern us, understanding how to

flow with life rather than struggle against it. We can return to our natural state of contentment.

The five principles will teach you to live in a positive feeling state more of the time. Use them as a navigational tool to guide you through life and point you toward happiness.

PART ONE

The PRINCIPLES

CHAPTER ONE

The Principle of
THOUGHT

All that you achieve and all that you fail to achieve
is the direct result of your own thoughts.

— James Allen

HUMAN BEINGS ARE THINKING CREATURES. Every moment of every day, our minds are working to make sense out of what we see and experience. While this may seem obvious, it is one of the least understood principles in our psychological makeup. Yet understanding the nature of thought is the foundation to living a fully functional and happy life.

Thinking is an ability — a function of human consciousness. No one knows exactly where thought comes from, but it can be said that thought comes from the same place as whatever it is that beats our heart — it comes from being alive. As is true with other human functions, thinking goes on whether we want it to or not. In this sense, "thought" is an impersonal element of our existence.

The Relationship between Thought and Feeling

Every negative (and positive) feeling is a direct result of thought. It's impossible to have jealous feelings without first having jealous thoughts, to have sad feelings without first having sad thoughts, to feel angry without having angry thoughts. And it's impossible to be depressed without having depressing thoughts. This seems obvious, but if it were better understood, we would all be happier and live in a happier world!

Virtually all the clients I have worked with over the years have begun their sessions like this:

Client: "I feel very depressed today."

Richard: "Did you recognize that you were having depressing thoughts?"

Client: "I didn't have negative or depressing thoughts; I just feel depressed."

It took some time before I recognized the problem in our communication. We have all been taught that "thinking" means sitting down to "ponder," to put in time and effort, as if we were doing a math problem. According to this idea of thinking, a person who wouldn't dream of spending six hours obsessing about a single angry thought could nevertheless feel quite "normal" thinking fifteen or twenty angry thoughts for thirty seconds at a time.

"Thinking about something" can occur over several days or within a passing second. We tend to dismiss the latter as unimportant, if we recognize it at all. But this is not so. Feelings follow and respond to a thought regardless of how much time the thought takes. For example, if you think, even in passing, "My brother got more attention than I did — I never did like him," the fact that you now feel resentful toward your brother is not merely a coincidence. If you have the thought, "My boss doesn't appreciate me — I never get the recognition I deserve," the fact that you now feel bad about your job came about as soon as that thought came to mind. It all takes place in an instant. The time it takes to feel the effects of your thinking is the same amount of time it takes to see the light after turning on the switch.

The ill effects of thought come about when we forget that "thought" is a function of our consciousness — an ability that we as human beings have. *We are the producers of our own thinking.* Thought is not something that happens to us, but something that we do. It comes from inside of us, not from the outside. What we *think* determines what we see — even though it often seems the other way around.

Consider a professional athlete who "lets his team down" by making a critical error in the last championship game before his retirement. For years after retiring from the sport, he dwells on his error for a moment here and a moment there. When people ask, "Why are you depressed so much of the time?" he responds by saying, "What a fool I was to make such a mistake. How else do you expect me to feel?" This person doesn't see himself as the thinker of his own thoughts, nor does he see his thinking as the cause of his suffering. If you suggested to him that it was his thinking that was depressing him, he would, in all honesty, say, "No it isn't. The reason I'm depressed is that I made the mistake, not that I'm thinking about it. In fact, I seldom think about it anymore. I'm simply upset at the facts."

We could substitute any example for our ex-athlete's error: A past relationship, a current one "on the rocks," a financial blunder, harsh words we said to hurt someone, criticism leveled at ourselves, the fact that our parents were less than perfect, that we chose the wrong career or mate, or whatever — it is all the same. It's our *thinking*, not our circumstances, that determines how we feel. We forget, moment to moment, that we are in charge of our thinking, that we are the ones doing the thinking, so it often *appears* as though our circumstances are dictating our feelings and experience of life. Consequently, it seems to make sense to blame our unhappiness on our circumstances, which makes us feel powerless over our lives.

We Are the Thinkers of Our Own Thoughts

Unlike other functions or abilities that we have as human beings, it's hard to remember that we are the thinkers of our own thoughts. It's easy to remember that our voices are the product of our ability to speak. It would be virtually impossible to startle ourselves with our own function of speech because we are so aware that we are the ones creating the noise. We could scream and yell and rant and rage, but we still wouldn't be frightened by the sound of our own voice.

The same could be said about our ability to ingest and digest food. You wouldn't eat something and then wonder why you had a certain taste in your mouth — you are always aware that you are the one who put the food in your mouth.

But thinking is different. William James, the father of American psychology, once said, "Thinking is the grand originator of our experience." Every experience and perception in life is based on thought. Because thinking precedes everything and goes on so automatically, it's more basic and "closer to home" than any other function we have. We have innocently learned to interpret our thoughts as if they were "reality," but thought is merely an ability that we have — we are the ones who produce those thoughts. It's easy to believe that because we think something, the object of our thinking (the content) represents reality. When we realize that thinking is an *ability* rather than a *reality*, we can dismiss any negative thoughts that pass through. As we do so, a positive feeling of happiness begins to emerge. If we harbor negative thoughts (pay too much attention to or dwell on them), we will lose the positive feeling and feel the effects of the negativity.

Here is a typical example of how thought can be misunderstood and how this lack of understanding affects us — the "thinker." Let us pretend that you accidentally spill a glass of water on the floor of a restaurant and look up to see that a man, two tables over, has flashed what you believe to be a disapproving look. You respond with anger. "What's the matter with that guy," you think. "Hasn't he ever dropped anything? What a jerk!" Your thoughts about the circumstance make you frustrated, and end up ruining your afternoon. Every few minutes you remember the incident, and as you think about it, you become angry. But the truth of the matter is, that person didn't even see you drop the water. He was in his own world, reacting to his own thoughts about an error he had made at work earlier that day. He couldn't have cared less about you. In fact, he didn't even know that you existed.

Unfortunately, all of us have experienced this kind of situation many times. We forget that we are only thinking. We fill our heads with false information, which we then interpret as "reality" instead of "thought." If only we could remember that *we are the thinker.* If we really could understand that as we think about something, we feel the effects of our thoughts, during this episode at the restaurant, we might have been able to recognize that it was our own thoughts, not another person, upsetting us.

To understand the principle of thought and how it applies throughout the human experience is a valuable gift. We need not constantly be in conflict with our environment and with those around us. We can maintain a positive feeling of happiness, because we no longer feel compelled to seriously follow every train of thought that comes into our heads. You may have no control whatsoever over what another person does, but you *can* be immune to the adverse effects of your thinking about him, once you understand that you think "thoughts," not "reality." Your thoughts, not your circumstances, determine how you feel. An absence of negative thought brings forth a positive feeling.

If you don't understand this principle, it may seem as though thinking is determined by what the outside world is doing. But it's actually the other way around. Our thinking shapes our experience of life. The way we think about something and, most important, *the way we relate to our thinking*, will determine its effect on us. The outside circumstance itself is neutral. Only thought brings meaning to a circumstance. This is why the same circumstance can, and will, mean entirely different things to different people. In our restaurant example, had you dismissed your negative thoughts, the incident wouldn't have mattered to you. In a healthy relationship to your thinking, you would have your thoughts, but you wouldn't "run with them" and allow them to upset you.

Our Relationship to Thought

A person's understanding of the relationship between thought and reality can be put on a continuum:

"My thoughts _____ "My thoughts
represent reality."   are only thoughts."

On one side is thought as "reality." Clinically, this would be a psychotic, a person who would never use the word *thought*. A psychotic actually experiences every thought as reality. To him there is no difference between thinking and reality. If he thinks he hears voices telling him to jump out the window, he tries to do it; if he thinks he sees a monster, he runs from it. Regardless of the content of his thoughts, he believes them to be reality, 100 percent of the time.

On the opposite end of the spectrum is the person who understands the thought process — a person who epitomizes mental health and happiness — a person who doesn't take his own, or anyone else's, thoughts too seriously — a person who rarely allows his thinking to bring him down and ruin his day. A person on this side of the scale can have any thought run through his head and still understand that "it's only a thought."

Most of us fall somewhere in between these two extremes. Very few of us take all of our thoughts so seriously as to be considered psychotic. Surprisingly, however, even fewer of us truly understand the nature of thought enough to fall on the far right of the scale. Most of us don't understand that we are the thinkers of our own thoughts — we do it to ourselves. Perhaps at times we see it, but only selectively. Our minds will create numerous exceptions to this principle, which keeps us from the understanding we need to implement it in our lives. For example, you might be feeling low one day and have the thought, "I'll never be able to finish this project." Rather than saying to yourself, "Oh there go my thoughts again," and putting an end to the negativity right then and there, you might continue on the same train of thought. You'll say, "I knew it when I started; I never should have tried this project; I've never been any good at this kind of work and I never will be," and so forth. Proper understanding of thought allows us to stop these everyday "thought attacks" before they beat us up. Recognize these types of thoughts as static on the television set —

as interference. There is no value in studying and analyzing static on a TV screen, and there is equally little value in studying the static in our own thoughts. Without a proper understanding of thought, the smallest amount of static in our minds can spiral and grow until it ruins an entire day or even a lifetime. Once you see your negative thoughts as static, interference, you can dismiss them — they are no longer serving your needs. In the example, the negative thoughts about your ability to finish a project are certainly not going to help you finish it.

We all produce a steady stream of thoughts, twenty-four hours a day. Once a thought is forgotten, it's gone. Once it's thought of again, it's back. But in any case, it's just a thought. In a practical sense, this suggests that to think about something doesn't mean we must take the thoughts to heart and react in a negative way. Pick and choose which thoughts you wish to react to.

Most of us are capable of understanding this principle for other people, but not for ourselves. Take the case of a frustrated freeway driver. Another car cuts him off and almost causes an accident. A thought passes through his mind: "I should shoot the driver of that car." What has occurred is a thought, passing through his mind. Most of us would dismiss it as a silly thought. We would all prefer that drivers be more careful, but we wouldn't take our violent thought very seriously. A psychotic, however, may not be able to dismiss the thought so easily. He fervently believes that any thought that comes to mind is reality and must be taken seriously.

While we can empathize (if not laugh) at the folly of

taking such a thought seriously, we all do the same thing, in different forms and extremes, hundreds of times each day. Each of us, in our own fashion, confuses our thinking with reality. We can see other people's thoughts (like the freeway driver's) as being "just thoughts," but we almost always fail to see our own the same way. And why do our thoughts seem so real? Because we are the one who creates them.

We Don't Always
Have to Take Our Thoughts Seriously

For one person, the thought, "I wonder if she likes me, I'll bet she doesn't," might cause distress. Yet this same person may recognize the freeway driver as "just having a thought." Most of us believe that if we have a thought, it's worthy of serious attention and concern, but if someone else thinks something, we might see it as just a thought not worthy of attention. Why is this so? Again, because thought is something that shapes our reality from the inside out. Because it is so close to us, it's easy to forget that we are the ones doing it. Thought helps us make sense out of what we see — we need it to survive in the world and to put meaning into life. When we understand the true nature and purpose of thought, however, we don't need to take to heart (or take so seriously) everything we happen to think about; we can lighten up.

Our thinking is not "reality," but only an attempt to interpret a given situation. Our interpretation of what we see creates an emotional response. Our emotional responses are not the product of what happens to us, then, but are derived from our thinking, our belief system.

To illustrate, let's use the example of the circus coming to town. For people and families who love the circus, this is great cause for celebration. For those who don't love the circus, the increased traffic and confusion causes concern. The circus itself is neutral — it isn't the cause of positive or negative reactions. We can think of many similar examples ourselves. Once we understand the concept, our thoughts can be a tremendous gift to us and help us with our lives. Conversely, we can become the victims of our own thinking, and the quality of our lives can diminish. Since our thoughts change from moment to moment, life can become a struggle, if not a battleground.

Our level of happiness seems to go up and down with our circumstances. In reality, it isn't the circumstances, but our interpretation of them that determines our level of well-being. This is why identical circumstances can mean different things to different people. Learn to see negative thoughts as a form of mental static, and you can stop paying so much attention to them.

Understanding the nature of thought allows us to live in a state of rest, a state of neutral, of positive feeling, happiness, and lighthearted contentment. When our attention is taken off what we are thinking about, particularly when it is negative, we are left with a nice, easy feeling. In no way is this meant to suggest that we don't need to think — we definitely do. It only suggests that negative thoughts — thoughts that cause distress and unhappiness — aren't worth dwelling on because they take away what we are looking for, a feeling of happiness. This contentment creates necessary space in our mind for new, creative thoughts to enter, allowing us to have that childlike quality of soft focus which brings back wonder and adventure to life.

This softer focus allows us to listen to people in a loving way. It enables us to listen even to criticism in a way that does not bother us because we're no longer analyzing — we're merely taking in information.

Ultimately, the relationship you have to your own thinking will determine your mental health and happiness. Do you believe that because you think about something, it must be taken seriously? Or do you understand that thinking is something that you do by virtue of being human, and that you need not confuse thinking with reality? Can you have thoughts and let them pass, in soft focus, or do you feel compelled to contemplate or analyze them?

Laura and Steve

Laura is driving to visit her boyfriend, Steve. Along the way she hears news on the radio about the number of marriages that end in divorce. She begins to think: "I wonder if Steve and I will get married. I wonder if it's worth it. How good would our marriage be? Steve has many of his divorced father's characteristics. He's often late and he tends to work too hard. I wonder if I'm as important to him as his work. I wonder if our children would be as important as his work." And she continues brooding.

Laura's thinking has gone on automatically. These

thoughts took place in an instant. Let's compare the effect of these thoughts based on her relationship to her own thinking. First, let's assume that Laura (like most people) believes that if something crosses her mind, it must be worthy of attention and taken seriously. She has no real awareness that she is *creating* the thoughts, but assumes that the content of her thinking must have relevance. She now feels justifiably concerned about her relationship and decides to bring up the issue with Steve. The remainder of her drive is spent worrying.

Now let's consider an alternative. Here, Laura understands how her thoughts create her experience of life. The identical thoughts pass through Laura's mind, and for a moment, she begins to feel the adverse effects of her thinking. Then she remembers that it was her *thoughts*, not Steve, that had her concerned about their relationship, which until that moment was perfectly fine. A few seconds earlier, before the news report, she had been reflecting about how well everything seemed to be going — she was in that nice feeling state where she was just thinking her thoughts, not analyzing them. She chuckles and feels grateful that she no longer has to be victimized by her own thinking. She initiates a softer focus and dismisses her thoughts. She spends the drive enjoying her favorite music and her happiness.

Having the Option to Act On Our Thoughts

Most of us assume that if something comes to mind, it does so for a reason; it must be representative of reality, worthy of our attention, and dealt with. If we understand the principle of thought, however, we know that this is a mental error. If something comes to mind, recognize it for what it is — a passing thought. This doesn't mean that we can't or shouldn't consider or act on the thought, but it does provide the option. Thousands of thoughts pass through our minds each day; as the principle of thought goes, none is more important than the next, each of them is just a thought. Once we understand this principle, what we think about will no longer have the power to completely determine the quality of our lives. Instead, we can choose to stay in the nicer feeling state that comes from a softer focus of thought.

The reason we can watch an upsetting or even horrifying movie and then go out for a meal is that we are always one step removed from the film. We understand that it's just a movie. Once the movie is over, it's over. It's no longer with us, we go on with our lives. The same is true with thought. It's only in our minds. Once a thought is out of mind, it's gone — until we think it again. There's nothing to fear from thought itself, once we understand that it's just thought.

Perhaps the greatest misinterpretation of this principle is to believe that the goal is to control what you think about. It isn't. The goal is to understand thought for what it is: an ability you have that shapes your reality from the inside out. Nothing more, nothing less. What you think about is not ultimately going to determine the quality of your life, but rather the relationship you have to your own thinking — the way you manufacture thoughts and respond to them. Do you hear your thinking as reality, or as thought?

A Dream Analogy

It's common to wake up in the morning and say, "Wow, that dream seemed so real." But, however real the dream seemed to be, we recognize it as a dream. So if we dreamed that we brought our car in to a mechanic to be fixed and he made the problem worse, we wouldn't go down to the service station and complain. We understand that dreaming is nothing more than thinking while we are asleep. When we apply the same understanding to waking thought, which seems real, too, while it's occurring, we no longer need to see it as truth.

The Two Aspects of Thought

There are two aspects of thought that are very important to understand. First is the fact that we think, that we have this human function — it's not what we think about (the content), but the recognition that we are the thinkers who produce the thoughts constantly going through our mind. The second aspect, the one that is usually discussed, is content, or *what* we are thinking about. There is a major difference between the two. Advocates of positive thinking suggest thinking positive thoughts as much as you can and avoid negative thinking altogether. While it's true that thinking positive thoughts will make us feel better than thinking negative ones, positive thinking is an erroneous concept, based on the assumption that thought, in and of itself, has a reality which we need to be concerned with. But be it positive or negative, thought is still only a *function*.

When we understand thought for what it truly is, we see positive or negative thoughts for what they are. A positive thinker is constantly under pressure to produce only positive thoughts, which takes enormous effort and concentration, leaving little energy for new and creative thoughts. When negative thoughts do enter the mind (which they will), a positive thinker has to deny their existence and override them with positive ones.

People who understand the nature of thought don't have the pressure to produce any specific content to their thinking. They see thought for what it is: a function of consciousness, a voluntary ability that shapes our experience of life. Does this mean that people who understand that thought is a function will intentionally think negative thoughts? No, of course not. Neither does it mean that negative thoughts will never enter their minds. They merely understand that negative thoughts, in and of themselves, have no power to hurt them. To them, thoughts, whether positive or negative, are simply thoughts.

Stacey's Story

Thought as a pure function of consciousness doesn't have any content until we put it in. Our beliefs, ideas about life, underlying assumptions, and opinions will determine the content we put into our thinking, but thought itself is harmless, an empty concept until we fill it with meaning. Suppose, for example, that when Stacey was a young child, her parents hired a live-in babysitter to help take care of her. When Stacey grew up, she believed that the most im-portant element of being a good parent was spending the most amount of time possible with her children. One day while she was reflecting about her parents, a thought came to her mind that her parents weren't as attentive as they might have been. After all, they had hired a live-in babysit-ter for her. Why didn't they want to take care of her them-selves? Maybe they didn't care about her as much as they said they did.

But how does she know that? What is she basing that conclusion on? Who just put the content into her thoughts about parenting? She did. A thought came to her mind about her parents — a simple thought to begin with, until she added the content that said, "Maybe my parents didn't care as much as I always thought they did." Never mind that Stacey had a perfectly healthy and loving relationship with both her parents — a thought has come to her mind. If she takes this thought seriously and runs with it, it will definitely lower her spirits. She could discuss it with her friends, her spouse, or if it seemed really important, she could even bring it up to her parents and take issue with them. In fact, popular psychology would have her do just that — analyze the static, then act on it. The idea of getting something off your chest and expressing your feelings is thought to be a good idea — but is it always? If Stacey understood where her feelings were actually coming from, would she choose to bring them up with her parents?

All this grief, and much more like it, comes from a simple misunderstanding of the nature of thought. Rather than see-ing her thinking as something that she was constantly doing,

Stacey tended to take her thoughts to heart. Had Stacey recognized what was happening, she could have dismissed her negative thoughts about her upbringing — allowing her to maintain a positive feeling and feel secure about her life.

The story of Stacey and the live-in babysitter will come up again in the next three chapters to demonstrate how the five principles work together to create a happy life.

Thought Systems

All of our past thoughts can be clustered into our "thought system," a self-contained unit through which we see the world. Every decision, reaction, and interpretation we have is colored by our individualized thought system.

Our thought system is like a filter that information passes through before it gets to our awareness. It is a complex, perfectly woven pattern of thought, linked together into concepts, beliefs, expectations, and opinions. It is our thought system that enables us to compare new facts or situations with what we already know from past experience.

Your thought system contains all the information you have accumulated over your lifetime. It is past information that your thought system uses to interpret the relative significance of everything that happens in your life. In this sense, a thought system is the source of *conditioned* thought. When you rely on it, you are thinking in a habitual manner, your *usual* way of seeing things. Here is where your habitual reactions to life are formed.

Thought systems contain our view of "the way life is."

They are the psychological mechanisms that convince us when we are right, accurate in our understanding, or justified. Thought systems by nature are stubborn and do not appreciate being tampered with. They are absolutely self-validating. If your thought system includes the idea that our country's schools are horrible and are the cause of most of our problems as a nation, then the following scenario would be possible: You're reading the evening paper and on page thirty-six, you come across an article near the bottom of the page that says, "Twenty-one students fail literacy exam in district." You smile; you are proven right again. You show the article to your spouse, "You see dear, our schools are falling apart. It's just like I've been telling you." You don't know that on the front page of the same paper, the headlines read, "NATION'S SCHOOL TEST SCORES UP 17% OVER THE PAST FIVE YEARS!" But such is the nature of thought systems. Due to the way they are wired in our minds, there will always seem to be a logical connection among things we perceive to be true. Our beliefs will always make perfect sense to us within our own thought system.

Our thought systems lead us to believe that we are realists and that the way we see life is the way life really is. The fact that one person can view a situation as an opportunity and another equally intelligent person sees the same thing as a major problem doesn't bother a thought system. Our thought system dismisses the other point of view as off track, well intended but wrong, or not quite right.

Because our thought systems are filled with our memory of the past, information we have accumulated throughout our lifetimes, they encourage us to continue to see things in the same way. We react negatively (or positively) to the same situations or circumstances over and over again, inter- preting our current experiences in life as we have in the past. A person who believes that people are inherently critical will become defensive whenever anyone offers a suggestion, regardless of whether the person meant to be critical. This will become a theme in his life unless and until he under- stands the nature of thought systems, particularly his own. Understanding this concept will help him see that he is not seeing reality, or truth, but an *interpretation* of reality through his own thinking.

Because our thought systems are so familiar to us, they seem to be giving us true, accurate information. Because of the self-validating aspect of thought systems, we accept fa- miliar ideas and disregard the rest. This is why people rarely change their political or religious views, and why they hesi- tate to even discuss them with friends or family. They "know the truth" and can come up with examples and argu- ments to support their claims. They also "know" that their family and friends "don't understand the truth," and be- cause they are stubborn, they probably never will. We know the result of locking heads with other thought systems — usually frustration is experienced on all sides. This is why people gravitate toward others who share their beliefs, and become impatient with those who don't.

Understanding the nature of thought systems can change this. When we know that other people (and our- selves) innocently interpret our beliefs as if they were real- ity, we can let go of the need to be right. We can see that our beliefs are merely a function of past conditioning and expe- riences. Had our past been different, our ideas about life would be different. Other people's beliefs are also a result of their past experiences. Had things been different, a totally different set of beliefs would have surfaced.

"This may be true," you say, "but my view of life is a good one and not only do I still think it's accurate, I wouldn't change it even if I could." The point here is *not* to change your thought system or your ideas about life, but to see the arbitrary nature of them. We only need to see the *fact* of thought systems, not tamper with the contents, to reduce the frustration in our lives. Unless we understand thought systems, we can rarely hear other points of view. We interpret what others say and do based on what we already know. Information comes in and we decide whether it makes sense, based on our previous knowledge. Unless the information is something we already agree with, our thought system will have a tendency to discount it. In short, new information is usually unwelcome within our existing thought systems. This is why we can be bothered by the same events or circumstances over and over again throughout our lifetimes. We have developed recurrent cause-and-effect relationships between certain events and reactions.

For example, you might believe that whenever someone gives you a suggestion, it means that they disapprove of you as a person. You won't question this because your thought system will validate it. It always seems to be a true, accurate assumption about human nature. Even if someone assures you that your assumption is off base, you convince yourself that the other person has hidden motives or that they are not aware of their hostility toward you. However long it takes, you will seek to verify your existing beliefs to prove yourself right, even at the expense of making yourself miserable.

But if you understand the nature of thought systems, you can begin to see beyond them, and sense the value in other points of view. What we used to interpret as criticism we now see merely as an opinion from another person with his or her own thought system. We can virtually eliminate unprofitable arguments in our lives and can completely eliminate feeling resentful, confused, or angry at others who don't see things our way. In fact, when we understand the stubborn nature of thought systems, we will expect others not to see things our way.

Bob and Carol and Ted and Alice

"Couple A," Bob and Carol, have an understanding of thought systems. "Couple B," Ted and Alice, do not.

Couple A, Bob and Carol, have a small child whom they both love very much. Bob, in an honest attempt to help relieve his wife of some responsibilities, offers to take time off to take their child to the doctor for his shots. He doesn't perceive this as the most joyous part of raising children, but nevertheless he is offering to do it. Carol, who believes that taking her infant to the doctor is an important way to show her love, appreciates her husband's offer to help and thanks him, but declines his offer. She knows her husband's thought system contains different ways of offering help than her own. More important, Carol understands that she has her own thought system, with its different needs, beliefs, and desires about mothering. She calmly decides she would rather do it herself.

Couple B: same scenario, different level of understanding. Ted, who cares about his child as much as Bob, offers the same help. Alice doesn't understand thought systems. To her, offering this kind of help is a statement that she isn't a good mother. She would never offer this type of help to her friends (except in an emergency) because she "knows" that taking your child for shots is a requirement for being a responsible mother. She responds to her husband by accusing him of not respecting her parenting skills. Since Ted has no more understanding of thought systems than she does, he calls Alice "an ungrateful person." An argument ensues and both the husband and wife end up unhappy for days. This is only one example of the typical arguments that can result from a lack of understanding of thought systems.

Had either Ted or Alice had this understanding, the argument would never have occurred. The wife would have heard her husband's offer and, regardless of how she felt, would have responded with, "No thank you. I'd like to go myself," or something to this effect. Had Ted understood thought systems, he would have nipped the problem in the bud by recognizing Alice's reaction as a function of her thought system. He would have been able to explain his desire to help in a nondefensive and loving manner. Even if she didn't respond to his loving explanation, he wouldn't have taken her assault so personally. Instead, he would have recognized that the problem was two thought systems playing ping-pong with each other, which is precisely what was happening. Two thought systems can't see eye to eye any more than two people speaking different languages can understand each other without an interpreter.

Interestingly, Carol felt as strongly as Alice about being the one to bring their child to the doctor. The difference in their behavior wasn't due to their opinions or their circumstances, but in their understanding. Carol knew that her opinion came from her thought system, but Alice believed that her opinion came from being a mother. She believed that certain duties inherent in being a good mother were more important than others, and she interpreted her husband's offer to share responsibilities as a criticism of her parenting skills.

When we understand how thought systems work, we can avoid this pattern of similar unnecessary arguments and the unhappiness it causes.

CHAPTER TWO ·

The Principle of
MOODS

Time cools, time clarifies; no mood can be maintained
quite unaltered through the course of hours.

— Thomas Mann

J UST AS WE ARE CONSTANTLY THINKING as human beings,
our level of awareness that we are doing the thinking is
constantly changing. This constant shifting in our awareness of ourselves as the thinker is what is known as changing "moods." Up, down, up, down, every minute, every day,
our mood level is on the go. For some people, mood shifts
are slight — for others, extreme.

In either case, the fact remains: we are never in one
place emotionally for too long. Just when it seems like life is
going smoothly, bam, our mood level drops and life again
seems rocky. Or, just when life seems hopeless, our mood
lifts and everything seems all right again.

When you're in a high mood, life looks good. You have perspective and common sense. In high moods, things don't feel so hard, problems seem less formidable and easier to solve. In a high mood, relationships flow easily and communication is easy and graceful. In low moods, life looks unbearably serious and hard. You have little perspective; it seems as if people are out to get you. Life seems to be all about you. You take things personally and often misinterpret those around you. These characteristics of moods are universal. They are true for everyone. There isn't a person alive who is happy, fun to be around, and easygoing in a low mood, or who can stay bummed out, defensive, angry, and stubborn in a high mood.

Our Moods Are Always Changing

People don't realize their moods are always on the run. They think instead that their life has suddenly become worse in the past day, or the last hour. Take the example of a client who came to me initially because he perceived himself to have serious relationship problems with his wife. He came to my office on two consecutive days. On the first day he was glowing, even bragging, about how much fun he'd had with his wife over the weekend. As he described it, they had laughed, played, talked, and taken romantic walks. Clearly, he was in a high mood. The next day he came in complaining about the lack of gratitude he felt from his wife for all he was doing for her. "She never appreciates anything I do," he said. "She is the most ungrateful person I've ever met."

"What about yesterday?" I asked. "Weren't you telling me how wonderful everything was between you?"

"I was, but I was dead wrong. I was deceiving myself and have been for our entire marriage. I think I want a divorce."

Such a quick and complete contrast may seem absurd, even funny — but we're all like that. In low moods we lose our ability to listen, and our perspective flies out the window. Life seems serious, important, and urgent.

Moods Are Part of the Human Condition

Moods are a human condition. You can't avoid them. You aren't going to stop changing moods by reading this book — this can't happen. What can happen is that you can understand that moods are part of being human. Rather than staying stuck in a low mood, convinced you are seeing life realistically, you can learn to question your judgment when you're in this state. You will always see life and the events in it differently, in different moods. When you are in a low mood, learn to pass it off as simply that: an unavoidable human condition that will pass with time, if you leave it alone and avoid giving it too much attention.

With an understanding of moods, we can learn to be appreciative of our highs and graceful in our lows. This contrasts sharply with what most of us do in a low mood — where we try to think, figure, or force our way out of it. But you can't force your way out of a low mood any more than you can force yourself to have a good time doing something you don't like. The more force (or thought) you put into it, the lower you sink.

Because life looks so serious in a low mood, there is an inherent sense of urgency within it. This is why most people have their serious discussions in low moods, and it is one of the core problems in relationships. The simple act of acknowledging a low state of mind, in ourselves or in others, can change the course of a relationship.

The same behavior by our children that is cute when we are in a high mood, is irritating when we are in a low mood. But once we understand the principle of moods, we will not confuse our children while we are in a low mood by unjustly accusing them — and then have to spend our time and energy when we are in a higher mood apologizing for our words or actions. This holds true in dealing with people other than our children, and in all situations. When we understand the power that our moods have on our perspective, we will no longer need to react to or be victims of them. Things will eventually appear to us very differently if we just let them be, for now.

Your Mood Changes, Not Your Life

A high mood, positive feeling state, healthy psychological functioning — "that certain feeling." In this state of mind, no mental adjustment needs to be made; you feel good. But what about those times when you don't feel so good? An understanding of moods allows you to get back to this healthy state quickly after losing it. When you understand that it is your mood — not your life — that has suddenly changed, you have a better perspective. This new perspective teaches you to take your thoughts less seriously when you don't feel good — to slow down your thinking and take your attention away from what you are thinking about. You will become more graceful and patient with your moods, which helps you get back to a state of healthy functioning.

Remember Stacey and the live-in babysitter? How might an understanding of moods affect that situation? If you look closely, you will notice that *all* situations like this are mood related. When Stacey drops into a low mood, like everyone else, she produces negative thoughts about life. In this example, she was producing negative thoughts about her parents, because of their decision to hire a live-in babysitter for her when she was a child. If you had asked her the day before, when she was in a higher mood (positive feeling state), whether she cared about this old issue, she would probably have laughed. She might even have said, "You know, that's a great idea, maybe I should try it with my child."

I am not discounting the fact that there are times when you will draw the same conclusions about situations irrespective of your mood. But the way you feel about something will always depend on your mood. Stacey might feel, even in a higher mood, that hiring a live-in babysitter is not a great idea for her, but she would not be as adversely affected by her thoughts.

It makes sense for all of us to be aware of our mood level, particularly when we are down. If Stacey had understood that she was in a low mood, she would have *expected* to react the way she did to her thoughts about her parents' decision. She would have *known* that she was having a low-mood reaction and that it would be best to reconsider her feelings when she was feeling better.

Everything looks different in different moods. If we understand this principle, our compassion for ourselves and for others increases dramatically. We will know that at times our partners or friends will see the bright side, the opportunity, in a situation, and at other times they will see everything as a potential or real problem. If you learn to recognize other people's moods, you will cease to judge them when they are seeing the darker side of life. In a low mood, we *all* see the darker side. An understanding of moods will allow you to remind yourself, "Of course they see it that way in a low mood." Without such understanding, you will see others as pessimistic, negative, or shortsighted. You forget that an hour ago, the same person saw the exact same circumstance in an entirely different manner.

When we begin to take notice of our own mood levels, suddenly the mood itself becomes responsible at any given moment for our outlook on life. In a higher state of mind we will see the same situation differently. This is not a cop-out to responsibility, but a fact of life that applies to every situation we have ever been (or will be) involved in.

Don't Take Low Moods Too Seriously

If we don't understand the power of moods, we will tend to take to heart what our partner (or anyone else) says to us.

Once we understand the principle of moods, we will see that this is an invitational setup for problems. The more time we spend with someone, the more likely we are to see them in their low moods. In a low mood, anyone could say things to us that we wish they hadn't.

Most serious relationship problems turn out to be nothing more than two partners who have made a habit of taking each other's low moods too seriously. The inevitability of our partner's outlook and behavior in low moods, the problems we were certain we had for so long, seem less formidable when we learn to pay careful, respectful attention to the mood level of our partners, and "let them be" in a low mood. So often, just letting others alone while they are in a low state of mind is all they need to pull themselves out of it and regain their own common sense and a more positive feeling. The last thing they need or want is someone questioning or arguing with them. Doing so will reinforce and deepen their mood, which will encourage more of the same. Most partners don't give each other the space they need in a low mood; instead they react as if what their partner is saying is carved in stone. It's not! When the person pulls out of the low mood, his position will soften and he or she will be easier to be around.

Once you experience this principle in action, you will be pleasantly surprised at how quickly and easily troublesome situations will resolve themselves. The key is to see that our partner's words and actions, as well as our own, are mood related. When we begin to see the truth in this principle, we won't be searching for alternative partners to replace the ones we already have. Instead, we will realize that anyone we meet, anywhere in the world, is going to have a fair share of low moods. Going from partner to partner, thinking that someone else would be better, loses its appeal: there is not a person alive who doesn't experience up and down moods. Learn to appreciate and understand the partner you already have — and learn to enjoy each new person you meet more.

While we can be compassionate and understanding of others in their low moods, in our own low moods we need to stop listening to ourselves. Despite the urgency we feel, in our lowest states we'll never see things in perspective. If something seems important right now, it will still be there when we feel better and more equipped to deal with it. The quickest way to a higher mood is to discount the way we feel in a low state. The quantity and quality of our thinking keeps us low. As we learn to disregard negative thoughts, our positive feeling will quickly return.

I'm not suggesting that only our high moods are representative of reality, or that our low moods are falsehoods. Both high and low moods will seem real and justified within themselves. When you're in a low mood, the way you are seeing things will always seem reasonable. In fact, you can't see them any differently. The trick is not to see it differently, but to recognize the state of mind you are in, and to understand that when you are in a low mood, you will generate negative thoughts. The same exact circumstance you are involved with today will look very different to you tomorrow, or perhaps even ten minutes from now. If you can drop your concern and wait out the low mood, your level of well-being will rise once again. As your feelings become more important to you than your thinking, the quality of your feelings will improve.

Don't Try to Solve Your Problems in a Low Mood

How many times have you heard yourself say, "That wasn't like me," or, "That couldn't have been me talking — I lost my head"? There's good news and bad news about this common tendency. The bad news is that it was you talking, just as it has been in the past, and as it always will be when you lose your perspective in the future. The good news is that it was only you in a low mood; it was low mood talking. Had your mood level been higher, your circumstances would have looked completely different and you would have behaved differently.

The good news, in a practical sense, is that from this point forth, you can recognize and acknowledge low moods whenever you are in them. Respect the power of a low mood, the certainty with which you see the dark, problematic side of a situation. Because of the nature of moods, you won't see things differently while you are in one. But you *can* learn to distrust yourself and the thoughts you generate when you wind up in low mood. If a genuine problem exists when you're low, don't worry — the problem will still be there when your mood level goes up. And when it does, you will be better equipped to deal with it. It doesn't make sense to put too much emphasis on what you think in a low mood — doing so will only keep you from a feeling of contentment.

Solve Your Problems in a High Mood

If we confront a person about something while that person is in a low mood, we can rest assured of the result. The person will become defensive, bothered, and nonreceptive. The same is true for ourselves. If we attempt to solve a problem or make an important decision while our mood level is low, we will likely disappoint ourselves and regret our behavior.

When our mood is low, we don't have access to our wisdom. The confusing part of this part of this principle is that *it is in our low moods that we will want to solve our problems and confront other people.* The seduction will always be there. Low moods breed confusion and resentment. They encourage us to "want to get to the bottom of something," "read into what others are saying," "work on our communication," and "express our feelings." But the feelings you have in a low mood are not your true feelings — they are the feelings that you (and others) feel in a low mood. The only feelings you will ever experience in a low mood are negative feelings; thus, it makes no sense to trust or act on those feelings. The solution is to wait until the mood rises, *which it will, on its own.* The less attention you give your thinking in your low moods, the quicker your mood will rise. At that point, and that point alone, your wiser feelings will surface.

Then even if you feel compelled to take some serious action, you will sense the most appropriate way. If you want to have a discussion about something that's bothering you, the time to do it is in a high mood. The principle of moods does not say to avoid confrontation — except when you're down. The principle provides the easiest, most graceful, most productive way to approach life.

Another confusion about the principle of moods is that sometimes while you are in a low mood, you think you have to confront people. While this is sometimes true, it's not as frequent as you might think. Often, a few minutes apart from your problem can be all you need to take the edge off. The mood is the *root cause* — not the effect — of most disagreements and problems. The mood came first. In a higher mood, the same scenario would have looked completely different.

On those rare occasions when you do have to confront someone while you (or they) are in a low mood, the most important thing to be aware of is that you are in a low mood and that your vision of the situation is suspect and limited as a result. This understanding allows you perspective.

Accessing mental health, like anything else, gets easier with practice. The more you trust that nice feeling of happiness, the easier it will be to stay with it longer. Practice ignoring your low moods, rather than analyzing them, and see how quickly they vanish. Low moods are a distortion in our thinking. Accept low moods as a part of life, do the best you can to ignore them, and healthy psychological functioning will be more prevalent in your life.

CHAPTER THREE

The Principle of
SEPARATE REALITIES

We don't see things as they are,
we see them as we are.

— Anaïs Nin

IF YOU HAVE TRAVELED to foreign countries, you are aware of vast differences among cultures. Even those who haven't traveled have probably seen television, movie, or book depictions. The principle of separate realities says that the differences among individuals are every bit as vast as those among different cultures. Just as we wouldn't expect people of different cultures to see or do things as we would, the principle of separate realities tells us that the individual differences in our thought systems prohibit this as well. It's not a matter of tolerating differences in behavior, but of understanding that it literally *can't* be any other way.

In the previous two chapters, we learned about two

major ways that people function psychologically, in thought and in moods. Because every human being functions in these ways, it's impossible for two human beings, from the same culture or not, to see things precisely alike. There are no exceptions to this rule. Each thought system is unique to itself. It is formed through a process of thinking that depends on input. Our parents, backgrounds, interpretations, memory, selective perception, circumstances, mood level — many factors play roles in determining our individual thought system. The combinations are endless, and impossible to duplicate between individuals.

Understanding this principle can virtually eliminate quarrels. When we expect to see things differently, when we take it as a given that others will do things differently, and when we understand that others will react differently than we do to the same stimulus, the compassion we have for ourselves and for others rises dramatically. The moment we expect otherwise, the potential for conflict exists. This is true on a small scale, between two people in a relationship, or on a large scale, such as relationships among nations. We can see examples of this principle everywhere. With our attention (thinking) off of our expectations, we are free to experience the unique essence of every person, bringing forth a nice feeling in ourselves, and maximizing the potential of our relationships with others.

It Is Futile to Try to Change Others

Problems in relationships come about in essentially two ways. We either think that others actually *do* see things as we do, so we can't understand or are upset by their reactions — or we believe that others *should* see things the way we do because we see reality as it really is. When we understand the principle of separate realities, we are free from these catalysts of relationship problems. Others not only shouldn't see things our way, but in fact they cannot. The nature of individual thought systems makes it impossible for us to see anything the way someone else does — or for others to see things precisely as we do. This new understanding frees us from a false idea and brings the joy back into our differences. It's one thing to say "variety is the spice of life," and another to really believe and understand it. The trick in believing this is not to force yourself to think this way, but to see that, from a psychological perspective, differences between people and the ways they see life make complete sense.

When you understand the fact of separate realities, there is no logical reason to take personally what others say and do. People spend their lifetimes proving to themselves that their personal version of life is valid, realistic, and correct. This self-validating aspect of thought systems will point to endless examples to prove itself right. When you understand this idea, you see the futility in attempting to change someone else, or in even arguing with them. If you argue, the other person is usually so certain that he or she is right that he or she may even use *your* facts to prove his or her position, as in the following example.

Let's take a husband and wife who have been married for twenty years — the husband sees people as generally critical by nature, and the wife sees them as being complimentary whenever possible. For years, they have been arguing this particular point, the husband pointing to endless examples of how people are critical and aggressive. For every example the husband comes up with, the wife has an equal number of examples to prove her position. Neither one can understand why the other is so blind to the "facts." One day, the two of them are at a restaurant and they overhear one waiter saying to another, "Did you see the hat on the woman at table two? Wow!" The wife immediately turns to the husband and says, "You see? There's another example of a person being complimentary. How nice! What's it going to take for you to see that it's true that people are looking for opportunities to give compliments to others?" The husband looks at his wife in shock and says, "Complimentary, what are you talking about? The man was laughing at the poor woman's hat."

This amusing misunderstanding is clarified in an instant when we understand the dynamics of what is actually taking place. All you need do is accept it as a given that each of us sees life from our own separate reality, our own interpretation of life, our own frame of reference. None of us questions our own version of reality because to us it always seems to be true. Everywhere we look, we see examples to continually prove ourselves right.

Separate Realities Is a Fact of Life

The key to coming to terms with and seeing the beauty in separate realities is to see the perfect innocence of the process. We see what we see based on our conditioning and beliefs (our thought systems). Your mind will interpret a set of circumstances in the context of what it already knows or believes to be true. Because you have unique knowledge and a unique set of facts from your past, your interpretation of any situation will vary accordingly. It's as if your mind was a complex computer system, and as with a computer, interpretation of data is dependent on previous input. So too with ourselves. Our minds process current information based entirely on previous knowledge. There's simply no way to avoid separate realities, and if we do not accept and understand this fact of life, we will be frustrated or perhaps even destroy our lives. With understanding, this knowledge can be a source of wisdom, joy, and humor.

Understanding separate realities does *not* mean you must forego your deepest opinions or beliefs. Beliefs and opinions in themselves are neutral. They are an interesting, enriching, powerful aspect of life. The important element in happiness, mental health, and personal contentment is your *relationship* to those beliefs and opinions. Do you believe that the way you see life represents the only actual and indisputable reality? Or do you understand that your present beliefs and interpretations of life are derived from your own thought system, and if the information contained in that thought system was different, your conclusions would be different? The idea is not to label particular beliefs or ideas as right or wrong, but simply to understand how ideas are derived, the inevitability of seeing things differently from others. When we understand the principle of separate realities, we can continue to maintain any belief or opinion we have — the difference will be that our personal beliefs, and other people's objections to them, will not be such a source of hostility or pain.

Defenses Will Drop and Hearts Will Open

The understanding of separate realities brings us undeniably closer to those we know and love. It helps us to understand others, and it also makes us much more interesting and accessible. When we truly understand that our ideas about life come about from our thought systems and do not necessarily represent reality, other people are drawn to us.

And here's why: All of us have a vested interest in validating our own beliefs. But thought systems (our own or those of others) don't like to be threatened or tampered with. When you approach someone, not in an attempt to change their beliefs, but with a genuine interest in and respect for their view of life, defenses drop and hearts open. People who wholeheartedly accept the fact of separate realities have more fulfilling relationships than they ever dreamed possible. Often, relationships develop with people whom you had come to believe you couldn't possibly like. Rather than being frustrated and angered by someone's individual differences, you begin to see that person in a new light, an innocence not only in them — but in yourself. The result is a softening of the beliefs of both people, a new appreciation of one another, and a nice, positive feeling.

The principle of separate realities can be represented by a continuum:

Intolerance ———— Tolerance ———— Understanding

On the far left of the scale is where most people believe that relationships develop problems. And they're right. As we move toward tolerance, problems are worked on, but hardly solved. While tolerance is certainly more desirable than intolerance, it represents a tiny fraction of where you need to be on this scale if you want happy, satisfying relationships. Tolerance of other people and their way of being in the world suggests a subtle form of superiority from our own position or viewpoint. From what you know now about thought systems and separate realities, you know that your own personal ideas about life and how life should be lived cannot be superior to anyone else's. The information in your thought system is every bit as arbitrary as the next person's. Your ideas, beliefs, opinions, and reactions to life are a product and function of the information and stimulus you took in, and this is equally true for people who see life diametrically differently than you do. If you don't understand this, the differences between people can become a major source of frustration. If you do understand separate realities, those same individual differences become a source of interest, growth, and inspiration.

Growth and Compromise Become Possible

Especially when differences seem insurmountable, the understanding of separate realities has immensely practical implications. If we approach another with understanding, it opens the door for growth. When we don't view other positions as inferior or wrong, we accept new information without our old thought system discrediting it. Without this understanding, our thought system takes over and prevents us from truly listening. Listen without judgment, and the person you are with will sense your respect for their position and your willingness to listen. The result is increased understanding and softening on both sides — the essence of compromise or collaboration, bringing out the best in ourselves and in others.

Let's return, once again, to Stacey's reflections on her parents' decision to hire a live-in babysitter for her when she was a child. If Stacey does not understand separate realities, it's no wonder she was upset at such a decision. After all, it was very different from her own beliefs about parenting! Because she believed so strongly in her own thoughts, she tended to brood on them, causing herself additional distress. When Stacey first reflected on her parents' decision, she did so without an understanding or appreciation of separate realities. She was unable to see why her parents would make such a decision. Additionally, she was equally bothered by other decisions and opinions that did not match her own viewpoints.

An understanding of separate realities would allow Stacey the luxury of reflection without irritation or judgment. She would know that her parents made the decisions they did based on what was true for them at the time — nothing more, nothing less. Stacey then wouldn't label her reaction right and her parents' decision wrong, but recognize them simply as different decisions, based on different thought systems. Stacey's relationship with her parents would be filled with mutual respect and love rather than doubts and accusations.

Not understanding the principle of separate realities can result in constant conflict and frustration. The solution is to gain an adequate understanding of this concept, and to have the humility to admit that you can't always step into the minds of other people. No matter how easily you see something, or how obviously true a situation appears, someone else will assess it differently and be equally certain of that position.

CHAPTER FOUR

The Principle of
FEELINGS

You are only one thought away from a good feeling.

— Sheila Krystal

YOU HAVE AT YOUR DISPOSAL a foolproof guidance system to navigate you through life. This system, which consists solely of your feelings, lets you know when you are off track and headed toward unhappiness and conflict, away from healthy psychological functioning. Your feelings act as a barometer, letting you know what your internal weather is like.

We recognize the powerful connection between our own thinking and our experience of life. When we think, we immediately feel the effects of our thoughts. It happens in an instant and, for most of us, without awareness that it is happening.

We think in one of two ways: either habitually, through our individual thought system, or through what is called a "natural state of mind" — healthy psychological functioning. We have discussed the effects of thinking through your thought system. In this chapter, you will see that you have another very real alternative.

The fourth principle states that our feelings tell us, with complete accuracy, when our thinking is dysfunctional. When we are not aware we are thinking, our thoughts are generated through the thought system, instead of through healthy functioning. If it were not for our feelings, we would never know when we were caught up in our thought systems or when we were in a low mood. We would be convinced that we were seeing life realistically, even in our lowest states of mind.

When we are not caught up in thought systems, our feelings remain positive. We have a feeling of contentment and a sense of joy in whatever we happen to be doing. There doesn't seem to be a rationale for the positive feeling; we just feel good. We experience the deeper, more generic, human feelings that are generated from a natural state of mind: contentment, love, and gratitude. This is a state in which we see life clearly. We have soft focus and concentration — our mind is clear. We can do anything in this state of mind (including unpleasant things) because our minds are not cluttered with thoughts of the past, the future, or judgments about how we are doing. We deal with whatever, or whoever, is before us. This is the state of mind from which new and creative ideas evolve, and where solutions to problems seem obvious. Each one of us has access to this state of mind, and when we are in it, no mental adjustment needs to be made — everything just flows naturally.

When our experience of life is other than pleasant, our warning system of feelings kicks in like a red flag and reminds us that we are off track. We have reverted back to thinking through our thought system. We are now thinking in a dysfunctional manner and it's time to make a mental adjustment.

Our feelings are to our mental health as the warning lights on our dashboards are to our automobiles. Both let us know that it's time to ease up. In the car, we ease off the accelerator. It's time to pull off the road.

Likewise, when we feel discontented, we need to clear our heads and stop what we are thinking — which brings us back to a positive feeling. Temporarily drop the thinking which is coming from a distorted and habitual frame of reference. Remember, dismissing or ceasing to listen to thoughts that are upsetting does not mean pretending that things don't bother us or need improvement. But a good solution or new ideas will never come about from dysfunctional thinking — only from a positive feeling state where life seems easy. We need to begin to discredit the validity of our thought system when it comes to maintaining and accessing our own mental health. Decide, once and for all, that negative feelings aren't worth defending and harboring.

The only value in negative feelings is to let us know that we are seeing life in a distorted manner. This idea is heavily contested in current psychological thinking. Many, if not most, psychologists today share the belief that becoming more aware of your feelings (whatever they are) and then expressing them represents emotional maturity. Nothing could be further from the truth. If your mood is the source of your experience, not the effect, when you are in a low mood or feeling badly, you will generate negative thoughts 100 percent of the time. If you feel badly and a psychologist (or anyone else) asks, "How are you feeling?" he or she is, in effect, asking you to explain how you see life when you are in a low mood. When your mood is higher, you will have a drastically different description of the very same events. There is no value in a low mood, except to remind you that you are thinking in a dysfunctional manner and shouldn't trust or seriously listen to yourself at present.

Distrust Your Feelings in a Low Mood

Remember, in a low mood, we will always be able to point to reasons why we feel the way we do and we will be tempted to trust our thoughts. But our thoughts in a low mood will be distorted, and because our feelings are a direct result of our thinking, so too will our feelings be distorted. Unpleasant feelings are an accurate indicator to let us know when we are thinking directly from our belief system — our habits, beliefs, the tapes that play in our heads.

This guidance system of feelings works perfectly, 100 percent of the time — trust it. It doesn't matter whether you are feeling stressed, overwhelmed, angry, depressed, lonely, frustrated, jealous, judgmental, or anxious. These feelings, and others like them, are there to tell you that you are looking at life through your thought system, not with your natural state of mind. If you continue thinking in the same unproductive way, you will not find the answers you are looking for.

When a warning light flashes in our car, the particular reason why it's flashing is not as crucial at first as the fact that *it is flashing*. The thing to do is pull off the road and turn off the motor. The way our feelings work is analogous. Whenever we are feeling angry, jealous, resentful, greedy, depressed, or in some way unhappy, we need to understand that these feelings are being manufactured by our own thought system and are not natural, accurate, or representative of reality.

Healthy Psychological Functioning

There is no magic or mystery to healthy psychological functioning: It is always present when we aren't engaged in our habitual thought system. Healthy functioning is the feeling we experience when little (if anything) is on our minds — a positive feeling state that exists for no apparent reason. Children possess this state of mind frequently, experiencing life simply, without putting too much negative thought into it. When they do experience negativity or frustration, they are able to let it go quickly and return to their natural state of happiness.

We've all experienced healthy functioning countless times since we were children. Perhaps it happened while you were sitting in front of a fireplace, taking a walk, or looking at a beautiful sunset — healthy functioning is present whenever you feel wonderful for no particular reason. The important point is that the fireplace or the activity didn't cause your good feeling. What happened was that you temporarily relaxed, cleared your mind of concerns, and simply took a few moments to enjoy your life. If you think you need a fireplace or a particular activity to clear your mind, you will be able to relax and be contented only in certain situations. Once you understand that it's yourself, and not the fire or the sunset that is producing the positive feeling inside, you can clear your mind at will. It becomes easier as you practice it, I promise you.

Healthy Functioning Doesn't Depend on Our Circumstances

We all have access to healthy functioning whenever we want it — once we know that it exists independent of our circumstances. This knowledge allows us to feel good even when things aren't going well. As long as our minds aren't focused on our concerns, we will remain in healthy functioning and maintain our sense of well-being. In this positive feeling state, we will be equipped to deal effectively with any aspect of our lives. The moment our mind shifts out of this state and back into our thought system (which will remind us of our concerns), we lose our sense of well-being and again see life as a series of problems to overcome.

Your feelings are the barometer that tell you whether

you are experiencing life from your thought system or from your natural state of mind. If you are feeling depressed, angry, or frustrated, these feelings tell you that your thinking is dysfunctional, that you are not experiencing your life as it could be lived. Drop whatever you are thinking, ignore the static, and make the mental adjustment to clear your head. Shift gears from your computer mode to your transmitter mode — from your thought system to your healthy functioning. Remember, you are only one thought away from a good feeling.

One Final Visit to Stacey

Let's return one final time to Stacey and her reflections about her parents' decision to hire a live-in babysitter when she was a young child. Because Stacey didn't understand the true purpose of her feelings, she innocently believed that because she was feeling badly, there must be some value in thinking about why she felt the way she did. She believed that her thinking must be telling her the truth about her parents. As she continued to brood about it, she felt worse and worse until she was convinced that her negative feelings were justified and that she had a right to be angry.

Had Stacey understood the true purpose of her feelings, she would have used them as a warning signal. Her feelings of resentment and anger wouldn't have continued because she would have realized that she was thinking in a habitual and dysfunctional manner that was leading her straight toward unhappiness. She would have dropped what she was thinking about, or had the wisdom to pay less attention to herself and return to a nicer feeling state. In this nicer feeling state, she could continue to reflect without the danger of ruining her day (or week), or damaging her relationship with her parents.

Whenever we are experiencing life from our most natural state of mind, we will feel happy. We will be able to do this irrespective of what is going on around us — even when we are grieving after the loss of a loved one. When we access our healthy functioning, emotional pain has a different feeling to it — it is still painful, but it includes genuine gratitude for having known the person we have lost. This worked beautifully in my own life, when one of my best friends was tragically killed by a drunk driver on his way to be in my wedding. Rather than think about him sadly, I was able to clear my mind and feel tremendous gratitude for having known such a wonderful friend. Instead of feeling sorry for myself or for my friend's family, fond memories began to surface from our past together. I was not overwhelmed by my sad feelings and was able to function.

As you incorporate these principles into your life, you will still feel all the tender, natural human feelings you have felt in the past. The emotions that will change are the ones that immobilize your life — those that keep you from living the vital and meaningful life you are capable of. What *will* change is your relationship to your emotions. Rather than feeling overwhelmed by them, you will experience them with understanding. In instances such as grief over a loss, it is perfectly natural to feel profound sadness. Accessing your healthy functioning allows you to experience even the difficult emotions with compassion for yourself, an understanding of what is happening inside you. Use the principle of feelings as a navigational tool to help heal and guide you back to where you want to be.

So what do we do when we feel angry, depressed, or anxious? How do we stop feeling these emotions and return to healthy functioning? Trust and see the truth in the principle of feelings. When we understand where our negative feelings come from (habitual thinking), there is no need to defend or hang on to them. How can we defend something we know to be arbitrary? Negative feelings will disappear quickly enough if we simply let them alone. They are created by our thoughts — to focus on them or analyze them will only extend and deepen the negative experience.

As our appreciation of and experience with healthy functioning deepens, we see that we shouldn't refer to our thought systems to solve important issues in our lives. Wisdom and common sense come from a more positive feeling state — from a quiet and rested mind. When we feel good, we are more equipped to solve any problem that may come up.

When you understand where your positive feeling state comes from, and stop pursuing negative feelings as a viable route to problem solving and happiness, you naturally gravitate toward your healthy functioning and begin to discredit, more and more, your negative feelings. As you do, you notice that the negative feelings you do experience are less severe, and don't last as long as they once did. You are able to gravitate away from these states of mind more quickly.

Once you understand healthy functioning, you are no

longer tempted to analyze or think your way to happiness. Happiness is already with you — only it is covered up by your negative, static thinking. Instead of thinking your way to happiness, just stop thinking about things that bother or anger you. Put your attention elsewhere to elicit your natural positive feeling state. This doesn't mean pretending that things don't concern you; it only means understanding where your positive and negative feelings come from.

Understanding where our feelings come from allows us to use them as the directional guide they were meant to be. If our internal experience of life isn't pleasant, we know that we are creating our own misery, via our own thought system. We will recognize and value our alternatives — making the mental shift to drop concerns, stop habitual thinking, and return to a natural state of well-being.

CHAPTER FIVE

The Principle of the
PRESENT MOMENT

M UCH HAS BEEN SAID ABOUT "living in the moment." Virtually every spiritual teacher throughout history has suggested this solution. In fact, this may be one of the oldest and wisest pieces of advice for living a happier life. Yet, despite all the emphasis on this advice, very few people seem able to implement this critical principle in their daily lives. I believe this seemingly simple concept is so elusive because the untrained mind is much like a puppy — it wanders off without realizing where it's going! Before long, the puppy (like our thoughts) gets away from us.

Of the five principles discussed in this book, this is the one your therapist is least likely to have shared with you. After all, much of therapy is spent discussing your childhood and other issues surrounding your past. And while you can certainly gain some insight into your present life by understanding your past, doing so is almost always taken to excess. Keeping your attention riveted to the past (or future) can become an insidious habit that's difficult to break. Many therapists actually encourage their clients to live in the past (or in the future), without realizing they are doing so and certainly with no intended harm. If you've ever been in therapy, you are undoubtedly familiar with the practice of encouraging a client to "reexperience" the past. Therapists prompt clients — sometimes harshly — to focus on, think about, and most frequently, discuss in great detail the past. This is done *instead* of teaching clients how to bring their attention back to the here and now — the only way to experience true happiness. In addition to focusing on the past, clients are encouraged to "get in touch with" the negative feelings that accompany their negative thoughts of the past.

In chapter 1, we explored the relationship between thought and feeling — the idea that every negative feeling is a direct result of thought. Thus the notion that it's a good idea to spend considerable time in the past — intentionally or otherwise — is very questionable. Doing so guarantees a great deal of negative feeling, which only reinforces that there really is something of substance to be concerned about, thus justifying your negativity and feelings of victim- ization. Stirring up negativity keeps you tied to your learned thought system and your habitual ways of thinking, and greatly reduces your ability to experience and access your wisdom. When your attention is mired in the past or future, it's predictable that your quality of life will diminish instead of improve.

On the other hand, when your attention is primarily in the present moment, the bulk of your experience comes from a place of wisdom rather than reactivity. Although you will feel content when you focus on the present moment, you won't repress or deny anything that's truly relevant. The thoughts and memories you *need* to grow as a person (even the painful ones) will surface at the appropriate time: when you have the ability to handle them and the inner resources to know what to do with the information you receive. Wisdom is like a built-in emotional monitor. It helps you keep your bearings and your perspective. It directs you toward happiness without encouraging you to pretend that things are different than they actually are. Wisdom does allow for negativity, but only when it's necessary and appropriate — a far cry from the negativity typically generated in a therapy session.

The only way to experience genuine and lasting contentment, satisfaction, and happiness is to learn to live your life in the present moment. Regardless of your past experiences, the specifics of your current circumstances, how much you analyze your past or speculate about your future, you will never be happy until you learn to live in the present moment. A mind that is "out of the moment" is fertile ground for worry, anxiety, regret, and guilt. This doesn't mean that every moment of your life should (or ever will) be spent focused in this moment, only that it is important that this occurs more often than not.

Dr. Wayne Dyer, who was kind enough to write the foreword to this book, demonstrates the importance of living in the moment with a wonderful and powerful story. He suggests imagining yourself on a boat in the ocean, and asking yourself three very important questions. The first: What is the wake? The wake, of course, is the trail of water left behind as you move forward. The second question: What powers the boat? The answer here is that the present-moment energy of the engine is the power that makes the boat move — not yesterday's energy, not tomorrow's, but the energy generated in the present moment. Finally, ask yourself: Can the wake power the boat? The obvious answer here is an absolute no! The wake is powerless. It was created by past energy and has no power in this moment. You see nothing more than the trail.

How this story applies to your life is fairly obvious but extremely important in understanding the pursuit of your happiness and your dreams. Many people live as if the past is the power running their lives. The truth, however, is that just like the wake of a boat, your past is powerless. It's certainly true that what happened in your past and the challenges you faced in your childhood *did* happen, and you *did* have to confront those challenges. It's also true that what happened in your past contributed to the way you see life today. However, that's where its relevance ends. Your past, as it actually exists today, is nothing more than the thoughts you have about it — nothing more, nothing less. In reality, your past is *all* thought — simple memory. This doesn't diminish your past or suggest that you should pretend it didn't occur exactly as it did. Seeing your past as nothing more than harmless memory allows you to keep your attention in this moment by freeing you from the compulsion to follow each train of thought that enters your mind. When you understand memory for what it really is — simple, harmless thoughts passing through your mind — rather than a present *reality* that must be analyzed and battled against, it's far easier to dismiss the hundreds of future- and past-oriented thoughts that run through your mind every day.

Understanding the harmless nature of your thinking reminds you, as I suggested in Principle One, that it isn't something that happens to you but rather something that you create — from the inside out. Once you see your thinking as an ability that can work for you or against you at any given moment, you'll be less frightened and bothered by your thoughts. You'll keep them in perspective. As thoughts enter your consciousness, you'll have a choice: You can look at them and respond, or simply let them go. It's up to you. When you empower yourself in this way, you'll become far less reactive and it will become much easier to remain in the present moment. Your mind won't view the specifics of your thoughts as front-page news.

When your thoughts are distanced from the present moment, whether you are thinking of your childhood or something that occurred earlier this morning, you are actually recreating your past through your thinking. As long as you are aware that *you* produce your thoughts, that *you* are the thinker, you can avoid feeling sad, angry, or victimized by bringing your attention back to the present. You won't assume, as many do, that if a thought appears in your mind, it must have done so for a really important reason, and now that it has, you're stuck with it. Instead, you'll remember that thoughts of the past are nothing more than actively engaged memories. And memories, much like dreams, are simply thoughts running through your mind. You need not be concerned.

The *only* way a thought, or series of thoughts, can harm you is if you give them significance. If you don't, they have no power to hurt you. And as long as you remember that your thoughts have no power to hurt you without your consent, you will retain power over your life. Rather than feeling victimized or defeated by the thoughts that stream through your mind, you'll be able to keep them in perspective. As thoughts enter your consciousness, you'll decide whether to pay attention to them, take them seriously and respond accordingly, or simply dismiss them and go on with your day.

The destructive effects of thought happen only when we forget that our thinking is simply a function of our consciousness — an ability that we human beings have — that doesn't need to be blown out of proportion. When we keep this bit of wisdom in mind, we realize that it's our thinking, not our circumstances, that determines how we feel. This gives us the confidence to live in the moment by removing the fear that we must pay such careful attention to our own thinking, or else. Others may have experienced a nearly identical set of circumstances as you, and they may feel depressed and resentful about their plight, while you feel quite content. Obviously, the difference in how you feel won't have anything to do with who was better off, but will be determined by who more clearly understands the nature of thinking and who takes it more in stride.

Understanding our thinking in this way allows us to live more of our life in the present moment by allowing us to become far less preoccupied with our thinking. When our mind spins forward toward worries and concerns — or backward toward regrets and past hurts — we can actively observe our mind and make gentle mental adjustments, suggesting to ourselves that we bring our attention back to the present. We can say to ourselves, "Whoops, there I go again," or something else that keeps our thinking in perspective, reminding us that we just need to slowly bring our attention back to this moment to bring back a feeling of contentment.

In Principle Four, we learned that our feelings tell us, with absolute accuracy, when our thinking is dysfunctional or when it's affecting us in a negative way. Similarly, our feelings are extremely helpful in detecting when our mind has slipped from the present moment. It's pretty likely, for example, that when we are feeling bothered, annoyed, or frustrated, that our thinking has somehow wandered from the present. The next time you're stressed or frustrated, take a quick, honest look at where your thoughts are. Almost certainly you'll be thinking about all you have to do in the future, or everything you did earlier in the day, or of something unpleasant that happened or may happen tomorrow. Rarely, when you are upset, will your thoughts be centered in the present. Most of the time, the present moment is quite peaceful. To explore this idea, try this simple exercise:

Stop reading for a moment and simply observe where you are and what you're doing. You're reading a book of your own choosing. You're either sitting or lying down. Hopefully, you're comfortable. Now, imagine your life right now — without thinking, for the moment, of what's wrong or what's lacking. You're just right where you are, reading.

Now, observe what happens when you inject a few thoughts about all you still have to do today or tomorrow. Watch what happens as you think about a few problems and complications. Bring to mind a few serious issues. By now, your peace of mind has been disrupted by your own thinking. The more you continue with your injection of future or past concerns, the more upset and frustrated you will become.

This short exercise can remind you of how powerful your thinking really is. Your thoughts can take you, virtually instantly, from a state of calm in the present moment, into a state of turmoil — without any actual changes taking place. The solution to this mental sabotage is to become aware and conscious of your mind spinning forward toward problems, deadlines, and issues — or backward toward reliving old wounds or frustrations. You need not pretend that the issues aren't or weren't there — you only need to be aware when your thinking is engaged in this mental dynamic. Simply become aware. You can then remind yourself to guide your thoughts back to the present when they are too caught up in problems. After a while, you'll begin to sense that most of life — that which exists outside this moment — is simply a part of your imagination and thinking. Learning to live in the moment is sort of like getting behind the wheel of a car for the first time. All of a sudden, you're in charge of where the vehicle will take you. As you become more proficient at living in the moment, you'll be able to decide, moment to moment, what your experience of life will be.

Pay attention to your feelings. They are there to help you; they are your friend. When you feel *off*, take notice. Gently observe your thinking. Where is it? If your thoughts aren't in the here and now, rather than being hard on yourself, or getting too much into the details of your thinking (analysis paralysis!), simply direct your attention back to the moment. Don't allow your thoughts to pull you away from happiness.

By now, you're undoubtedly seeing the interconnectedness of all five principles. They weave together like a beautiful tapestry to explain the mental dynamics of happiness. An understanding of moods, for example, plays a critical role in learning to live in the moment. One of the key reasons people find it so difficult to remain in the present moment is that they don't understand the power of their own moods, or how to respond when they are low. As I alluded to earlier, if you believe what you think when you are low, you will become too frightened or bothered to remain in the present moment. Low moods always produce negative, insecure thinking. In your low moods, you will feel an urgent need to get away from how you are feeling. I suggested the best way to deal with low moods is to distrust and ignore your thoughts — put them on hold — until you feel better. This is not denial. If you have a legitimate issue to face when you're feeling low, it will certainly still be there when you're feeling better. But you will be far better equipped to deal with it. Life will always seem easier with your wisdom in hand. Your life (and everyone else's) will always seem serious, urgent, and full of problems when you are feeling low. You must expect this and be prepared to make minor mental adjustments, such as ignoring, dismissing, and taking less seriously your thoughts during these low times.

The vast majority of us fall prey to an insidious tendency: trying to figure out our lives and problems when we are feeling low or in a bad mood. The nature of figuring something out takes you away from the present moment and into thinking, "What am I going to do?" You either become engaged in past-oriented thinking or anticipatory thinking. And, of course, the more caught up in your thinking you become, the farther from the moment you will be carried.

One of the surest secrets of happiness is to learn to relax when you feel down or stressed — having faith that the low period and accompanying feelings will pass if you do nothing. Your reaction to the urgency you feel keeps stress in place. So the obvious solution is to ignore or dismiss the thoughts you have while feeling low.

To a happy person, the formula for happiness is quite simple: Regardless of what happened early this morning, last week, or last year — or what may happen later this evening, tomorrow, or three years from now — now is where happiness lies. Happy people understand that life is really nothing more than a series of present moments to experience, one after another. They understand and appreciate the past for what it taught them about living more in the now, and they see the future as more present moments to experience. Mostly, they understand that right now, this very moment, is where life is truly lived.

A related formula for success: When you focus your attention in this moment, instead of moments that are over or yet to be, you'll maximize your productivity, creativity, and ability to accomplish your goals. Too many future-oriented or past-oriented thoughts cloud your vision and distract you from what you are doing. The more present-moment oriented you become, the easier it will be to stay on track, get focused, concentrate, and achieve your goals. In short, an undistracted mind is able to make wise, appropriate decisions.

Thoreau said, "Above all, we can not afford to not live in the present. He is blessed over all mortals who loses no moment of passing life in remembering the past." I couldn't agree more. I think you'll find that mastering this principle is remarkably simple. It just takes a little practice. Beginning today, start observing where your thoughts are focused. Are you engaged in what you are doing right now? Or, have your thoughts drifted toward the future or the past? You'll probably catch yourself drifting away dozens, even hundreds, of times a day. Don't worry. Pretty soon, this number will diminish substantially. You'll discover that when you are engaged in this moment, you'll feel happy and satisfied. This positive reinforcement will give you the faith to continue your practice.

A Brief
REVIEW

T HOUGHT, MOODS, SEPARATE REALITIES, FEELINGS, and the present moment — the most important thing to remember about the five principles isn't the principles themselves, but the direction that they are pointing. They point away from obsessive thinking about problems and people, and lead us to a quieter place inside, to nicer feeling. They don't encourage us to "not think," but to remember that thinking is a function that originates inside of us.

Because of this understanding, we can cultivate a healthy relationship to our thinking: a relationship that allows us to think our thoughts without also being bothered, troubled, overcome, or frightened by them. Because we understand the nature of what is going on inside our heads, the principles guide us to a sense of patience with ourselves and with others. They remind us that we all function in the same way and because of this, we can make allowances for ourselves and for other people. The principles serve as a road map that guides us toward a more positive feeling — the feeling of love.

If we are thinking about something that is causing us distress, the principles remind us that we can turn our attention away from that focus and toward a feeling of contentment. This nicer feeling isn't the result of having thought through the details of a problem to a satisfactory conclusion, but is derived directly from what we call healthy psychological functioning. This is the happy feeling that results when we think not from our individual thought system and habitual frame of reference, but from a mind at rest. Healthy functioning not only feels good, but provides us with fresh ideas about life and problem solving.

In the next section we will discuss how an understanding of the five principles can be woven into those areas of life that are often viewed as inherently difficult. With an understanding of healthy psychological functioning, you will move through life more gracefully, with a sense of joy and appreciation.

PART TWO

Applying the
PRINCIPLES

CHAPTER SIX

RELATIONSHIPS

My friend is one whom I meet,
who takes me for what I am.

— Henry David Thoreau

RELATIONSHIPS ARE DIFFICULT for many people. Yet once we understand the nature of relationships and how the five principles are woven into this understanding, our contact with others will cease to be a problem and will bring greater gifts.

Any relationship begins with us. When we can tap into a more positive feeling state ourselves, we open the door for mutual respect, open and honest communication, and a genuine sense of love. When our own lives are full of contentment, we have some left over for other people. When we feel good ourselves, there is no need to be overly critical or defensive, because we no longer feel threatened by others.

Everyone you come into contact with is doing the best that he or she can in life. No one is getting up in the morning with the intent of ruining your life (except perhaps some very disturbed people). People are genuinely trying to do the best they can to make their lives and the lives of others work out well. Most people, particularly those close to us, would welcome the opportunity to help us make our lives run more smoothly.

Everyone functions psychologically in the same way. We all think. We all have moods. Because our thinking and moods are unique to each one of us, we each live in a separate reality. And we all have feelings. These four psychological components are true of people everywhere in the world. They are true of you, your partner, your co-workers, your children; they are true of me, my wife, my daughters, my clients; they are true of everyone.

Consider the principle of thought. Each of us is constantly thinking, and we will do so for the rest of our lives, an impersonal element of life that goes on whether or not we want it to. Rain or shine, thought marches on, in ourselves and in others. How do we use this ability to our best advantage?

The Thought Systems of Others

We have learned that thoughts with recurring patterns become part of our individualized thought systems. Because our thought systems are self-validating systems (in psychological terminology, "closed systems"), we are unable to question them, and it will always seem to us that we are seeing life accurately and realistically. Because of this and because self-validating systems are very protective of themselves, we tend to question the ways in which others live their lives and do things. Information that doesn't match our existing beliefs will be filtered through our belief system and judged as "inconsistent with the truth," "a strange way of doing things," "weird," "unusual," "different," and most often, "wrong."

As we get to know another person better, this tendency to question their thought system will increase, not decrease. The more opportunity we have to interact and spend time with other thought systems, the greater is the chance of conflict. This is why the most difficult relationship for so many people is marriage. For unmarried people, the most difficult relationship is commonly with the person they are closest or most intimate with. In some ways, it seems ironic that we should be most bothered by those to whom we wish to be closest. But it can't be any other way, unless and until we understand the psychological functioning of ourselves and our partners. Once we do, the opposite will happen. With understanding, we will gain new love and respect for those we choose to spend the most time with. We will retain our positive feelings for them as special and unique people. The issue of our differences will cease to bother us — perhaps it will even become amusing! We will begin to see people as characters, rather than adversaries.

It's critical to know and understand that our partner (or anyone we are in relationship with) sees life just as clearly as we do. *No one* can question his or her own vision of life, because thought is the originator of our experience.

As we look at life from the inside out, our vision passes through our thought system, and it will always seem to us that *anyone*, if they weren't so blind or stubborn, would see things as we do. But they can't and never will be able to — in order to have consistently positive relationships, we must take this as a given.

Coming to terms with this realization is both a humbling and a freeing insight. On the one hand, we have to admit that what we have always called "life" is not life in its most accurate state. Our personalized version of life and our interpretation of others is arbitrary. Had the information that has been stored away in our memory and thought system been different, so too would be our vision of life and our reactions to others.

The good news is that your version of life isn't wrong. Yours is every bit as justified as anyone else's, because psychologically we all function in the same way. When we understand each other in this manner, we *expect* to see things differently from others. Because we learn to expect it, we are surprised and always delighted when someone sees something exactly as we do. And when they don't, that's okay. We learn to say to ourselves, "Oh, that's how they do it in their world."

I am not suggesting that we pay no heed to our differences or pretend that things don't bother us. If that's how you're feeling, please reread the chapters on thought and separate realities. Our thought systems are neutral. We can't pretend that they don't exist, nor is there any chance of eliminating them. The best we can do is understand that we (and everyone else) have them and that they determine what we see. With this understanding we can begin to listen to ourselves with a grain of salt — with wisdom and a sense of perspective. We can learn to take ourselves and *our* personal thoughts less seriously. As our understanding deepens, we will *genuinely* be not so bothered by others, and we won't take their thoughts so personally or seriously. We may completely disagree with someone else, and that will be absolutely fine. We don't have to see eye to eye with people, as we now have a new perspective.

Nurture the Good Feeling in Your Relationships

The most important aspect of a nurturing relationship is the feeling that exists between two people. If the feeling is good, we say we have a good relationship. If the feeling isn't so good, if the good feeling has diminished, we say we have a bad relationship. All relationships begin with some degree of positive warmth and feeling. The positive feeling is the reason the relationship went forward in the first place. The feeling was there because the people involved weren't thinking critically about each other! If you don't focus your attention on the negative aspects of a person, your natural feelings of love and respect are able to come forth.

The feeling we have inside of us will always affect the person we are talking to. For example, you could say to your child, "Of course I love you, I'm your father." If you say this with a harsh tone, your child will not take your words literally — he or she hears, and feels, the tone or feeling behind your words. There are many such examples that we experience every day. Whether we are talking to our children, our spouse, our partner, our friends, our boss, our employees, or a complete stranger, the feelings behind our words, not the words themselves, will determine how the other will interpret and react to us.

The way to get back your warm feeling for another is first to understand its importance and *make it a priority*. When you feel warmly toward another, you overlook your differences to a large extent. When you do have differences to work out, you do so calmly, from a place of wisdom. When you don't feel warmly toward another, you are reacting directly from your habitual thought system, continually pointing to your differences and blaming them for your discontented feelings. But as we have seen, it's *not* our differences that create our feelings, but our thinking that creates our feelings. Understanding our own thinking can release us from its ill effects.

The second aspect of regaining our positive feelings for others is to see the innocence in, and to look beyond, people's bad behavior. Beneath our negative behavior, we all want to be a warm, friendly, compassionate person. I've yet to meet or work with a person who doesn't see himself as a good person, or at least, as having the potential to be a good person. Even people who appear aggressive, stubborn, and selfish see themselves (or wish they could) as nice people.

The principle of moods teaches that each one of us operates as if we were really two people. At our best, we have access to our wisdom and common sense. We are friendly, helpful, and kind. But at our worst, our sense of equilibrium is lost. We stumble, tend to be negative, and exaggerate faults in others. The factor that determines where we are at any given moment is the degree (or lack) of insecurity we are experiencing within.

Think about yourself for a moment. How do you act and think about life when you feel insecure? Are you happy-go-lucky, at ease, and full of positive rapport? Of course not. Well, everyone, including the people we are in relationship with, functions in exactly the same way. When we understand and have the humility to accept this fact about human beings, we can make allowances for people's behavior. No one is at their best when they feel insecure.

Think about someone you know whom you perceive to be an offensive or demanding person — someone you have difficulty maintaining a positive feeling toward. Now, despite your difficulty, you know there are people who feel warmly toward that person. How do they do it? Are they blind to the facts? No. They do the same thing we all do for people we care about, without even knowing it. They look *beyond* the person's behavior. The person they like is not a static personality, set forever in stone, but someone whose behavior fluctuates according to his level of insecurity. They say, "Oh, Jim didn't mean what he said. He tends to lose his temper, and sometimes he says things he shouldn't." They see Jim, whereas you look at Jim's *behavior*.

We are all capable of looking beyond another's behavior, and do it all the time intuitively. We dismiss or defend the actions of people we love when we understand that they are feeling insecure. To improve our relationships, we need to do the same thing with intention, to have a warm feeling for someone even though we don't feel they deserve it. As we practice this, our rapport and feeling of mutual respect will increase.

The importance of this positive feeling in relationships can't be overstated. If we learn to access this feeling, we will bring out the best, not only in ourselves but also in the people we are with. The question isn't whether or not our partners will ever feel insecure again and act in ways we don't like. They will. The important lesson is to be able to *maintain* our positive feeling for them. If we can, it will help increase their self-confidence, and as their level of security goes up, their behavior will improve. Everyone wins! They will appreciate your compassion and love and will have learned from the experience. If, on the other hand, we can't maintain our positive feelings for our partners, their level of security (already low) will tend to drop even further. As their insecurity increases, their behavior will remain distasteful (or become worse), and their feelings will remain sour.

In poor relationships, people make the mistake of taking negative behavior personally. As we begin to sense the ease, common sense, and practicality of maintaining our positive feelings for others (even in adversity), both the number and severity of instances in which we feel attacked will diminish. Other people will sense our good feelings toward them and feel reassured, with resultant closeness and good feeling.

There is an old saying, "It's not what you say but how you say it." The "how you say it" is the feeling behind what you say. Look for a positive feeling inside you *before* you speak, if you want the interaction to be positive. Even if you feel you are justified or have real reason to be upset, still, wait for a better feeling to surface. When it does, your response will always be more appropriate and effective than it would have been before. This doesn't mean waiting to think of something nice to say, but instead just waiting for a positive feeling to come about. When the positive feeling surfaces, and it will, what we say will take care of itself. It may be nice, if that's what's appropriate, or it may not be. But if you wait for the positive feeling to be there before you speak, your relationships will greatly improve.

In those extreme instances where it seems impossible to find a warm feeling, understand that what's inside you affects the person you are with. You do have it in you to feel warmly despite bad behavior, to bring forth your wisdom and compassion. This, in turn, generates respect and understanding, which takes the edge off mutual frustration. You both will see the situation with clearer eyes and a broader perspective.

Rather than getting stomped on because of our "easy-going nature," we will begin to receive more of what we have been looking for all along: love and respect from others and from ourselves. People respect and admire others who are understanding of their mental state (especially when they are down), and they appreciate those who can maintain a sense of well-being when others have "lost their heads." Who would you rather be around — a person who gets upset and panics, or someone who keeps cool and is able to make the best of any difficult situation?

The extent to which we are *unable* to generate a positive or warm feeling for someone is the extent to which we are thinking negatively about them — now, or in negative memories. If we drop these thoughts or memories, our positive feelings for the person return. Although it may feel normal, it is not natural to feel negativity, frustration, or irritability toward another. When you do, it is a signal that you have reverted to looking at life and other people through your habitual thought system.

Think a moment about what would happen if you were arguing with someone you love — and right in the middle of the argument, a fire broke out in your home, putting your lives in danger. What would happen to your argument? It would cease to be important. It would be temporarily forgotten, replaced with thoughts of survival and concern for each other. Getting each other to safety would be your only concern. The feelings between the two of you would change instantly, in response to a change in your focus.

Many parents have had similar psychological experiences with their children. One minute they are angry — thinking about how late the child is in coming home, for example — and the next moment they are grateful their child is alive, after a phone call relating a serious accident that almost killed their child. We have all heard of or experienced such incidents.

In both examples, the individuals involved forgot what they were angry about, which created a change in their feeling for the person they were upset with. Perhaps the most powerful example of this is when one member of a couple with a rocky marriage is diagnosed with a terminal illness. Instantly the couple realizes the absurdity and waste of feeling anything other than love toward their partner. The years of arguing and bitterness are forgotten, and a sense of warmth and compassion returns to their relationship.

This new understanding about the care and feeding of relationships puts us in a precarious position. We now know too much about our psychological functioning and can't turn back, at least not all the way. We have to choose between regaining a more positive feeling in ourselves and improving our relationships — or continuing to think in a dysfunctional manner that makes us feel discontented.

I am not referring here to positive thinking or forcing ourselves to think of something nice, but to the fact that the very act of thinking is creating our misery or lack of happiness. You have the right to continue thinking anything you wish, for however long, but once you understand how thinking creates your moment-to-moment experience of life, you will undoubtedly decide to discontinue those thoughts that are taking you away from where you want to be.

Do I Want to Be "Right" or "Happy"?

If the most important element in our personal relationships is the feeling that exists between us and our partner, then being right isn't relevant, not if it diminishes the love we feel toward another person. When we understand the way in which our belief systems encourage us to validate our own rough interpretations of life, we learn that the same is true for everyone else. If we already know this, we won't have to argue or to be upset over our differences.

As the happy feelings between people increase, the

issue of right or wrong seems less significant. We still can maintain our opinions or preferences, but know that these opinions stem from our thoughts, not from eternal truth. Our positive feeling becomes more important than our opinions. As our appreciation of happiness in relationship increases, we take notice of the things that tend to take us away from this feeling. One major catalyst taking us away is the need to be right.

An opinion that is taken too seriously sets up conditions that must be met first before you can be happy. In relationships, this might sound like, "You must agree with or see my point of view in order for me to love and respect you." In a more positive feeling state, this attitude would seem silly and harmful. We can disagree, even on important issues, and still love one another — when our own thought systems no longer have control over our lives and we see the innocence in our divergent points of view.

The need to be right stems from an unhealthy relationship to your own thoughts. Do you believe that your thoughts are representative of reality and need to be defended, or do you realize that realities are different as seen through different eyes? Your answer to this question will determine, to a large extent, your ability to remain in a positive feeling state.

Everyone I know who has put positive feeling above being right on their priority list has come to see that differences in opinion will take care of themselves. A more positive feeling state allows us to see other positions, to listen with a finer ear, and to express our own beliefs in a more compassionate and caring way. (We might even learn something!) It allows us the luxury of not caring so much if it turns out that we can't agree.

Moods in Relationships

Each of us might feel like we're living the life of Dr. Jekyll and Mr. (or Ms.) Hyde. When we are in a good or high mood, other people seem nice. We see the beauty in relationships and we have a sense of perspective and wisdom. We have the ability to compromise, to see other points of view, and to maintain a sense of humor. We have loads of common sense and know instinctively what to do when adversity strikes.

In our low moods, we lose our perspective (or bearings), and life itself seems hard and frustrating. Our relationships seem to be a burden and other people seem irritating, or in some way out to get us. In low moods, it seems an affront to us when people don't see things as we do, and we have a sense of urgency and doom. In a low mood, every problem looks like just the tip of the iceberg to a much greater problem.

When we're in a high mood again, there is little on our minds. Life and our relationships seem to flow and somehow work out in a nice way. When our mood drops, our minds are again filled with concerns. It is in our lowest moods, when we are least equipped to do so, that we are tempted to try to solve problems or resolve issues with others.

Understanding moods in ourselves and in others is

critical if we wish to maintain harmonious and gratifying relationships. If we are in a low mood and it doesn't register, watch out! We'll be looking for trouble without knowing it because life will appear urgent.

If our built-in warning signal (our feelings) goes off (low mood), and we understand what happens when we are in that state, we will instinctively postpone discussing problems and concerns (if we can). We can't make good decisions in this state of mind since we aren't seeing others as they really are or seeing situations clearly. In our present mood, we are defensive, stubborn, angry, and narrow-minded, four surefire keys to a negative relationship. In a higher state of mind, problems don't appear to be so serious, and knowing this will result in shorter, less severe low moods that are uncomplicated by poor decisions or overblown reactions.

You can't avoid low moods, but if you recognize when you are in one and understand what happens, just sit back and wait for a more positive feeling to surface before responding to issues of importance.

Here is a practical example of how this understanding helped to nullify a potential source of disharmony in my life. I found myself in a very low mood. I was tired and had been working all day with clients. Somehow, nothing had seemed quite right all day. When I got home, I immediately received an emergency phone call from someone who wanted to talk about a problem. All I wanted to do was sit alone in a hot bath, or maybe hug my wife or daughter, but this person went on and on.

Before I understood about moods, this scenario would

have driven me crazy! I would have reacted with anger and frustration, and ended up first overreacting and making harsh decisions, then later either apologizing for my behavior, or, if I felt particularly stubborn, I would feel righteous — my "right to be angry." I would take at least part of my frustration out on my wife without even knowing I was doing it. But that day I recognized that I was in a very low state of mind, and I knew everything sounded worse now than it would later. So I listened to the information as best I could and told the person I would consider his options and get back to him. I set the information aside in my mind, knowing I would come back to it when my mood was higher. Sure enough, several hours later, after not thinking about it, I found myself feeling much better and the answers seemed obvious.

It's important to remember that if we perceive a real problem in a low state of mind, the problem *will still be there* when our mood level is higher. And we will be far more able to deal effectively with any adversity when our mood is higher. One additional point is very important. I don't deny there are times when you simply can't wait for a better mood to evolve. There will certainly be times when a higher mood would provide better answers and the patience or wisdom needed to solve a problem. We can't force a good mood, but if we understand moods, this isn't a problem. We simply do the best we can, knowing the state of mind we are in. Had I needed to make an immediate decision in the above example, I would have done so knowing that I wasn't seeing the situation with a clear head. I would have known that if the situation seemed to be an emergency, given my state of mind, I would have made the best decision I could, knowing it wasn't under ideal conditions. Being aware when you are in a low mood actually helps you make a better decision than you would if you assumed (erroneously) that you were seeing life (and the facts) accurately. If you have compassion for your own state of mind, your positions will soften. This is an important part of wisdom and self-knowledge when making a decision in a low mood.

It's important to know when we are in a low mood, and also important to know when others are in a low mood. For most of us, it is not difficult to sense someone else's mood level, particularly those we are closest to. In fact, someone else's moods, particularly the low ones, are often easier to detect than our own. After sensing a low mood in another, understand and respect the power of moods enough not to be concerned or personally affected by them.

When people we know, love, or work with are in a low mood, they have no sense of humor or perspective. Our spouses, co-workers, children, employees, friends, and others will say and do things in their low moods that they wouldn't dream of saying or doing in their high moods. If we didn't understand moods and their effects on people, we would be bothered or hurt by their misguided actions or comments.

Does this mean we should excuse negative behavior? Yes and no. It's not a matter of looking the other way, or pretending it doesn't bother you, but of allowing a human being who has moods to be a complete human being. Strongly reacting to someone else's low mood behavior is like reacting to bad weather, something that's beyond our power to change. (We would certainly prefer people to be less defensive or critical in their low moods, of course!)

What we *can* do is to take our understanding of moods out into the world and set a positive example. We can learn not to take other people's low moods so seriously, or take to heart what they say and do in these moods. You judge the situation, then bring forth the necessary compassion to help pull others out of a low mood and into a more productive state of mind.

While we can't singlehandedly pull someone out of a low mood, if we maintain our own equilibrium and sense of happiness, we will be helping them. Our partner's low moods will be shorter and seem less severe if we are not seriously affected by them.

Don't try to give people advice when they are in a low mood! None of us is receptive to information in a low state of mind. Don't ignore them either, but just understand and have compassion. The rest will take care of itself.

Separate Realities in Relationships

The principle of separate realities suggests that no two people see life in precisely the same manner. We all look at life through our own unique filter, our thought system. And while many of us know this at an intellectual level, the principle of separate realities reminds us that this is not merely an *intellectual*, but a *psychological* fact. Once we accept this truth, we become free to genuinely enjoy and learn from each other's differences, including those we may not understand.

Since each of us has our own personal frame of reference, our individual perceptions of life will vary. It will always seem to us that we ourselves are seeing a situation with a realistic outlook, but the principle of separate realities does not credit or discredit any one point of view, or argue right and wrong. It points out simply that reality is an apparition, how something *appears* from a particular frame of reference. Separate realities mean that each of us is like a foreign country!

Person A is certain the world is a safe place. Person B believes the world is dangerous. Who is right? Both are — within their own personal frame of reference. Both can point to endless, valid examples of why their viewpoint is correct and both would do so with absolute certainty.

When we see how our individual thought systems work to create our perspectives on the world, we are free to expand beyond those limitations. We feel less threatened when someone disagrees or is disappointed with us, because we understand the inevitability of this dynamic. We see the innocence in our own negative thinking and beliefs, as well as the innocence in the negativity of others. We recognize beliefs as the result of past conditioning. Our understanding of separate realities allows us to take things less personally, because we understand the nature of biases, beliefs, and philosophies about life.

When it is a given that we all view life differently, we can expand ourselves to see this as rational and beautiful, and open the door to more fruitful, mutually nurturing relationships. We will naturally become less defensive and less critical, because we are less attached to preaching our personal life view and more concerned with bringing forth universal positive feeling.

CHAPTER SEVEN

STRESS

Second thoughts are ever wiser.

— Euripides

MOST OF TODAY'S stress management professionals would tell you that they have "stressful" jobs. Because we live in a stressful world, the best we can hope for are better methods of coping: such is the thinking of modern psychology. Stress is a "fact of life" for most people — a harsh reality that must be dealt with. Stress is so popular that other people are offended if we don't appear to be under stress ourselves. Stress is seen as a necessary part of achievement, relationships, careers, and life. The word has become a catchall to describe, validate, and explain almost everything that is wrong in our lives. "If I weren't under so much stress, my life would be better" is a very common belief indeed.

Stress is a major cause of unrest in our lives, but we don't have to surrender our lives to it. If we understand where stress originates (in our own minds), and its relationship to our thinking, we can begin to eliminate it, regardless of our circumstances. Stress is nothing more than a socially acceptable form of mental illness, and can, to a large extent, be eliminated.

Stress is not something that "happens to us," but rather something that develops from within our own thinking. From the inside out, we decide what is and is not going to be stressful. Gambling may be a thrill for one person, and for someone else the cause of a nervous breakdown. For one person, having children is the purpose of life, and for another it seems like too much responsibility. Working with rape victims for one person is a worthy cause, and for another it causes anxiety. Each of these examples, as well as every other situation in life, is actually neutral, not inherently stressful.

The moment we define stress as coming from anywhere other than from within ourselves, we set ourselves up to experience it — and are too late to prevent it. Each time we describe stress as "out there," we validate its existence. We then need to find ways to cope with, manage, or manipulate whatever it is that we believe is causing the stress. So, for example, if we believe it is inherently stressful to be in a relationship with someone who works evening hours (or long hours), we will look for ways to cope with that situation. We might spend energy attempting to get our partner to change his or her career. Then, when our partner resists, we say, "See, I knew we had issues to deal with. I knew this was a stressful situation."

Or we might take a completely different route and commit ourselves to working on the relationship. We attend classes and workshops, read books, or see a marriage counselor in the attempt·to deal with our stressful relationship.

Whatever our strategy, we are validating the need to cope with the situation — which is only stressful because we defined it that way. We never stop to question our assumption; all the classes, workshops, books, and counselors we sought out assume that our initial assumptions were correct, and that we do indeed need to learn to cope with stress. With each class we take or each book we read, the belief that we are in a stressful situation will be reinforced and create more stress as a result. The more we think about it or attempt to change it, the worse it will seem, because we are validating that the stress exists outside of ourselves.

The same pattern develops and deepens whether we believe stress comes from our jobs, the world, our relationships, our financial situation, our backgrounds, the political environment, or anything else. If we don't understand where stress originates, we will either look for ways to change the so-called "source" (our environment, for example) or we will search for ways to cope. In either case we are fighting an endless battle. If we can't change our circumstances, we can continue to use that as an excuse for our unhappiness, and if we do manage to change, this validates our false belief that we had to do so in order to live a happy, stress-free life. Then the next time something isn't to our liking, we will think we have to change the circumstances again, engaging in an endless negative loop of stress.

Suppose you assume that being busy is inherently stressful. If you can't rework your schedule, you're out of luck — destined to feel stress forever! If you *can* change your schedule, you have really compounded the problem — not solved it — because now you have validated (in your own mind) that your assumption is correct ("I must change my schedule in order not to feel stress in my life"). Even if it was a good idea to reflect on and possibly change your schedule, the next time you feel stress you will assume the same thing, that you have to alter your circumstances or your environment in order to feel better.

You cannot effectively deal with something that, in reality, does not exist. Stress does not exist — other than in your own thinking. Your stressful thoughts are no more real than your nonstressful thoughts; they're still just thoughts. To rid yourself of the stress in your life, first understand that stress is your *perception* of the situation, not something inherent in it. There is not a "cause and effect" relationship between the events in your life and the feeling of stress.

For us busy people, there isn't necessarily a relationship between our schedule and the feeling of stress — after all, there are busier people than ourselves who don't feel that stress! It's not the schedule, it's the thinking of the people who have the schedule. Once you see there is no such thing as stress, only stressful thinking, you are on the road to immediate change and can take up responsibility for your own life. When you redefine stress as something you can control, it's possible to maintain a positive feeling, even when circumstances are a great deal less than perfect.

How Thoughts Grow
to Produce "Thought Attacks"

Our thinking is to our stress as water and sunshine are to our gardens: as we think about, dwell on, or focus on something, the object of our attention will grow in our minds. Our discontented feelings will seem more justified. If we perceive something as an irritation, we can turn that minor irritation into a huge source of stress if we think about it enough. This is why many people are so bothered by little things. If we don't understand the dynamics of thought, it's easy to blow things out of proportion.

You start with a thought: "I really don't care for Joann that much." Now that the thought has come to mind, one of two things can happen. You can either notice it, then disregard it as a passing thought, or you can focus on it and make it grow. If you disregard it, it's over and you're on to the next thought. Now you can calmly decide whether to spend more time with Joann and what action to take, if any. If you were to focus on the thought, it would begin to grow and you would feel its stressful effects. You'd notice that Joann has an annoying voice and some nasty habits. You think about the times she hasn't been a good friend to you, and has done things you didn't approve of. You have now developed a full-blown "thought attack."

You begin to feel a little angry and stressed out. "Who does she think she is, anyway?" You talk to your friends about her and see if they agree. Some do, some don't. You are drawn to talk only to those friends who share your sentiments about Joann. The ill feelings of others further justify your feelings, and pretty soon Joann is the "bad guy" who is causing your stress.

The same dynamics work in any circumstance or environment. We've all heard the classic story of how something as minor as the way someone squeezes the toothpaste can be a source of major discord in a marriage. In reality, the toothpaste, or the way someone squeezes it, has nothing to do with the crisis. Our focus on it and thinking about it is what causes the stress. The thought, "I wonder if my partner would mind squeezing the toothpaste differently," turns into a *series* of thoughts and connections to the past. "She always does things in an unorganized manner," "I'll bet she does it just to bother me," "This has been happening since the day I met her," "Everything she does bothers me," "There is probably a hidden meaning behind her actions," "I'll bet another partner wouldn't do this," "No one else has to put up with the things that I do," and so on. This train of thought happens instantly and automatically — for the most part without us even realizing we are doing it.

When people first hear this theory describing how stress works in our lives, they often believe that the solution for relieving it is a prescription for pretending that things don't bother us. I assure you it is not! It is, however, a prescription for genuinely not being bothered or immobilized by things that have always disturbed you in the past. As your understanding of this process deepens, you'll learn that dwelling on stressful thoughts makes you less effective at communicating your needs to others as well.

Most people can handle it when their partner suggests

an alternative way of doing something (provided that the person making the request is not experiencing stress himself). The less stress you experience or display, the more receptive others are to your needs. Conversely, the more stress you feel, the more demanding you will seem to others, making them less responsive to your requests.

Suppose you have a friend who is habitually late. Lately you have noticed that this "habit" has become worse and you decide to talk to him about it. If you feel angry, stressed-out, and bothered, and remind him of all the times he has been late, how disappointed you are, etc., you are likely to bring out a defensive response in your friend. He will sense your urgency and by no means will he listen or learn from you. Consequently, he will continue to be late — or perhaps even later.

If, however, you remain in a nice feeling yourself and calmly bring up the issue, the reverse might happen. You will have a receptive audience who will listen to you, and you will keep the respect and good feeling you already had from your friend.

The Details of Our Thoughts

The details, the specifics, of our thoughts feed our attention and can often compound the feeling of stress. If you are feeling in a low mood and have the thought, "I don't like my job that much," two things can then happen: You can simply dismiss the thought and/or decide to think about it later when you feel better. Or you can fill in the details — think about why you don't like your job, your boss, your commute, etc. Here, as is so often true, the details of your thoughts will snowball — increasing your feeling of stress. The better solution here would be to choose to empty your head of all thoughts about your job. Wait until later.

Contrary to popular opinion, thinking about why we feel bad, the precise way in which something bothers us, instead of releasing us, actually lowers our spirits and makes our perceived problems seem more formidable, not less. We can turn a simple feeling of uneasiness into a major source of stress in our life.

Suppose that in the supermarket a store clerk snaps at you to hurry up and write your check. Later in the day you tell a friend about the incident (a bad idea in and of itself). You report just how the person sounded, the tone of voice, the exact wording, the look on the person's face, how it made you feel, what you felt like doing in retaliation, and so on. As your description gets deeper and more detailed, it will seem as though the incident is occurring all over again. The way you felt during the incident is nothing in comparison to the way you feel now, despite the fact that the incident is over and you are now sitting with a friend attempting to enjoy each other's company. Because you now feel angry and resentful, it seems even more reasonable to talk and think about the incident even further. What's more, you are now certain that the grocery clerk is the cause of your stressed-out feeling! The vicious cycle seems never to end, because you are always at the mercy of everyone and everything. Unless and until the world conforms to your every wish and desire, you will continue to be upset. You have engendered this with your "thought attack."

To break this cycle, we must understand that it is our thinking that is creating our upset, and that we are the thinker who is doing it. If we weren't thinking about the supermarket incident, but instead were talking to our friend about something else, the clerk wouldn't be on our minds and would not be causing us stress. As we think of the incident and reproduce the situation, our thinking brings the incident back to life. Every detail we remember will further stimulate our feelings.

In order to combat this tendency, we don't have to use willpower or pretend that we never have negative thoughts. All of us have negative, angry thoughts enter our minds from time to time. What we can do is learn to ignore them more often. We can learn that we don't need to dwell on our negative thoughts, though we have probably done so many times before. If you have angry thoughts about the store clerk, see them for what they are: angry thoughts. You don't need to do anything with them — just let them go.

A Personal Example

Up until a few years ago, I believed that speaking to large groups of people was a very stressful thing to do. Each time I spoke to a group, I would notice and think about all the things that felt stressful to me. I would notice my perspiration and how nervous I felt; I would think, after the speech, about all the things I had not remembered to cover; and I would re-call people in the audience who didn't appear to listen to me. To top it off, I would read books about my "correct" assump-tion that public speaking was inherently difficult and stress-ful, and I would listen to friends, colleagues, and anyone else who would support my existing beliefs.

My conclusion, of course, was always the same: "I was right, speaking is very stressful." The more I thought about it, the more nervous I got and the more I built up speaking as the primary source of my stress. I had no idea that I was creating stress with my own thinking. I believed that speak-ing was inherently stressful and there was nothing I could hope to do about it other than get used to it.

The moment I realized that stress actually came from my own thoughts and beliefs about stress, I began to become a more effective speaker. I would think less about how I was doing and how stressful making a speech was going to be, and instead think about what I was going to say and how I was going to present the material. Rather than focus on those who weren't listening to me, I would concentrate my atten-tion on those people who appeared to be interested in what I was saying. Forgetting the pressure I imagined I was under, I would clear my mind and relax. My blood pressure dropped, I started having fun, and I became a much better speaker.

Healthy Psychological Functioning

Stress will always come about (irrespective of our circum-stances) when we take the things that we think about seriously

— and blow them up in our minds. For example, suppose your boss tells you that a new project is due in two weeks, and you have several other deadlines to meet as well.

Healthy psychological functioning would consist of taking this information in one ear letting it flow through your brain and right out the other ear. This would allow you to take the most appropriate course of action. Your response to the task at hand would vary, depending on how quickly you wished to get started. Healthy psychological functioning wouldn't allow you to clutter your mind with panicked, frustrated, angry, or self-pitying thoughts. Instead, it would allow you to see with a clear head the best solution given the facts.

Unhealthy psychological functioning (stress) would also consist of taking in the information, but instead of letting it flow through, you would have a "thought attack" — focusing on and analyzing the data to the point of frustration. You would end up saying, "I'm always under deadlines," or, "I'll never be able to get this done," or, "Why me?"

Unhealthy psychological functioning can turn even the smallest event into a personal nightmare. I once heard of a mailman who panicked and felt angry when his route was increased by two homes — from thirty to thirty-two! To most people this would have been a very manageable addition; to him, this was an extremely stressful situation.

The key to eliminating stress from our lives is to understand that we manufacture stress, just like our friend the mailman. Whenever we blow up anything in our minds, we create the potential for stress. Once we understand this psychological dynamic, we can begin to drop the thoughts that are interfering with our healthy psychological functioning and return to our most natural state, one of contentment.

The Purpose of Stress

Stress is an unpleasant feeling. Feelings are a directional guide, or compass, to let us know how we are doing psychologically at any given moment. Are we feeling a sense of contentment? Are we quietly happy with the task at hand? Or have we taken our own thoughts too seriously and trapped ourselves in our thought system?

The purpose of stress is to warn us when we are headed toward psychological danger. The more stress we feel, the more important it is to drop the thoughts that are on our mind. Stress can be a friend — by letting us know beforehand when we are headed away from happiness, away from clear thinking.

Physical stress shows these implications much more clearly. For example, if we feel a cold coming on (a small amount of physical stress), we may or may not decide to take the day off. As our physical stress increases, we pay closer attention to how we are feeling and make decisions that will encourage our stress to go away. So an athlete who sprains his ankle will probably decide to discontinue his practice in order to let his ankle heal. The worse the feeling, the greater is the need for rest.

Psychological stress serves an identical purpose. The more intense the feeling, the greater the need to slow down or stop not only what we are doing, but, more important, what we are thinking about. But for some reason, this isn't always obvious. In fact, when people feel stressed, that's usually when they roll up their sleeves and get to work. If they feel a relationship problem emerging, they try to "get to the bottom of it" or if something is on their mind, they become determined to figure it out; if there's work to be done, they put their foot on the gas pedal and step on the gas.

The dynamics of physical and mental stress work in exactly the same way. Just as when we feel ill, we're not at our best, so too, when we feel emotionally stressed, we're not at our best. When we feel stressed, we lose our psychological bearings, wisdom, and common sense; we tend to take things too seriously; we lose sight of the big picture and often get lost in the details of our problems.

Lower Your Tolerance to Stress

Surprisingly, the solution to stress is to begin to *lower* our tolerance to stress. This is the *opposite* of what most of us have been taught, but it is the truth. Lowering our tolerance to stress is based on the simple principle that our level of internal stress will always be exactly equal to our current tolerance. This is why people who can handle lots of stress always have to do just that.

People with extremely high levels of stress tolerance might end up with a stress-related heart attack before they begin to pay attention to what the stress is telling them. Others may end their marriage or find themselves in a recovery center for alcohol or drugs. People with lower tolerance might begin paying attention to their stress earlier, when their job first begins to seem overwhelming or when they find themselves snapping at their children. Still others, who can't tolerate stress at all, sense that it's time to slow down and regain perspective when they start merely having negative thoughts about their friends or family.

The lower our tolerance is for stress, the better off we are psychologically. When our goal is to feel our stress as early as possible, we can "nip stress in the bud" earlier, and return more quickly to a more positive feeling state. We have choices; in fact, we have a series of "choice points" in any situation. The longer we wait to disregard the stressful thoughts, the more difficult it becomes to bring ourselves back to our natural state of mind. Eventually, with practice, any of us can get to the point where we are aware of our negative thoughts before they pull us off track. Remember, you are just one thought away from a nice feeling.

This new way of understanding stress is not a prescription for laziness or apathy — in fact, it's the opposite. The more peaceful and happy we feel inside and the less distracted we are by our own thinking, the more productive and efficient we can be in all areas of our lives.

CHAPTER EIGHT

Solving
PROBLEMS

The common problem, yours, mine, every one's,
Is—not to fancy what were fair in life
Provided it could be,—but, finding first
What may be, then find how to make it fair
Up to our means: a very different thing!

— Robert Browning

T HERE ARE SEVERAL IMPORTANT POINTS to consider when attempting to solve any problem that comes up in life. In this chapter we will discuss how to solve problems using an understanding of the five principles of healthy functioning.

Typically, people think that solutions to problems come about either through a change of circumstances or through a laborious process of thinking. But there's another alternative — an understanding of problems that goes beyond "hit-or-miss" and applies generically to all problems. We will learn how to solve problems first by seeing the limitations in these typical approaches, and next finding out the most effective way to get over a problem or painful event.

Consider the typical notion that changing our circumstances is a major way to solve our problems. Obviously, there will be times in life when our circumstances are less than ideal. But it is also true that our view of our circumstances will vary in direct relationship to our mood and feeling level. We will see our circumstances in various ways depending on how we feel. In a low mood or feeling level, we might see our marriage as a trap or a burden. In a high mood or positive feeling state, we might see our marriage as a great partnership. In a low mood, we might see our job as boring and insignificant; in a higher mood, the same job is seen as satisfying, a viable, honest way to make a living. In both examples (as well as so many others), our circumstances haven't changed one bit. What changed was our mood level — our feeling. When we begin to see the relationship between our problems and the mood we are in, we understand that the answer to our problems won't necessarily be tied to changing our circumstances. When our mood and feeling level is higher, not only will we view the same circumstance in an entirely different light, but we will have answers to our problems that we couldn't see when our mood was lower.

Remember, mood is the source of experience, not the effect. In our lowest moods, we will always see problems and the reason why they exist. This will come as no surprise, once we understand the power that moods have on our perceptions; we will expect to generate problems in these lower states of mind. But we will know how to wait it out, rather than listen to or trust what we feel at the time. Our circumstances will look quite different once we feel better, and there will be fresh new answers.

Changing Circumstances
and Problem Solving

Circumstances are always neutral. If they were the cause of our problems, they would always affect us in the same way, which of course they don't. It's our thinking and perceptions about our circumstances that brings life to them.

Suppose you think that your partner is too critical of you. In the "change-the-circumstance" model of problem solving, the only viable solution is to try to change your partner's behavior. You bring up the issue of criticism, and your partner disagrees with you, saying, "You're just too sensitive." What now?

Round two — you bring it up again. This time, however, your partner isn't so philosophical, and accuses you of starting a fight. "You see?" you respond, "You're being critical again." And so it goes. Unless you can get your partner to change (which is usually very difficult), you simply can't solve the problem.

Consider another typical example. Your problem is the fact that you believe you are too old or too young to do something. Good luck in changing your circumstances — you can't! What if your problem is money (probably too little of it)? It's possible to change this circumstance, but what are you going to do in the meantime? Stay unhappy until you have more money?

In each of these examples, the problem is mood related. When you are in a low mood, you will see your partner as too critical, every suggestion as an attack. In a higher mood, the same words out of your partner's mouth wouldn't bother you at all. When your mood is low, some factor — your age, sex, race, or religion — will seem to inhibit your experience and cause you unjustified harm. In higher moods, you look beyond your characteristics and circumstances, and do the best with who you are. You will gravitate toward the activities that are most suited to you. In a higher feeling state, you will hear the elements of truth and concern for you in the suggestions other people make, instead of feeling offended.

In a low mood, if lack of money is a problem, it will appear that it takes a lot of money to do anything pleasurable or worthwhile. In higher moods, you won't think this way, you will find enjoyable activities within your budget, however tight it might be. *In higher feeling levels, we already have what we want to feel good*. The things we don't have seem unimportant, and we are grateful for what we have. We still pursue goals, but our pursuit doesn't run or ruin our lives. Instead we can gravitate toward what we want, while at the same time enjoying what we already have.

Our view of our individual circumstances will always change with our ever-changing mood and feeling level. So, while there are times when working toward positive change is appropriate, we need not be stuck with change as the only possible answer.

Almost everyone will go through periods of time when they feel they "don't like what they do." Many people fail to notice, however, that most of the time, they like what they do. Because they trust what they feel in a lower state of mind, they jump from one job to another, thinking that something else might bring them greater satisfaction. But in a low mood, this same person will not like his new career either. The same logic applies to other life situations as well.

It's much easier and more practical to wait for a changed mood than a changed circumstance. It makes sense, then, to postpone trying to solve problems until we feel good. In a more positive feeling state, we have access to our wisdom and common sense. When we feel good, the answers seem obvious, answers that were impossible to us in a lower state of mind. The same partner who drove us crazy an hour ago seems funny now. We find new ways to communicate; in higher feeling states, we might even see how our moods have been contributing all along to poor communication.

Your age, which an hour ago (in a lower feeling state) was causing you great distress, is now a nonissue. In a more positive feeling state, you see creative new ways to use your age to your advantage. You see your skills as unique. In a lower state of mind, it all seemed hopeless.

In a higher state of mind, you see new ways to produce income. You become more creative, insightful, and appreciative of your considerable skills. You see alternatives that were invisible to you when you felt low.

One of the keys, then, to solving problems, is to know that "feeling good" is highly practical. Feeling good comes first. Solving the problem comes later. This is the opposite of "change the circumstance," where happiness is dependent upon certain outcomes. Our ability to solve problems is tied directly to our ability to access our own wisdom and common sense, both of which come about from a positive state of mind or feeling state.

You only need to think back to the thousands of times your circumstances changed to realize that change alone isn't the key to happiness or to solving your problems. If it were, we would all be happy and problem free already! But we aren't. All of us have had our circumstances change for the better: we have received diplomas, jobs, approval, promotions, awards, or similar kudos which we thought were going to make us happy. But shortly after we received them, we lost our happiness again and began searching for better ways to change our circumstances and better our lives.

The way out of this psychological trap is to understand that problems are generated more by the way we feel than they are by our circumstances. The moment we stop trying to change circumstances and focus instead on raising our feeling level, our problems will begin to fade away. People who live in a state of happiness see answers that never appeared to them in lower states of mind. They become more capable of dealing with any challenge because they cease to waste energy attempting to solve problems in a state of mind where there are no viable answers.

Analyzing Our Problems

The "analytical" method people frequently use to solve problems involves intense deliberation, in hopes of coming up with a solution. In this approach, we try to think, figure out, make sense of, and analyze our problems.

The nature of problems, however, is that we are usually "stuck" on something. We somehow can't see the answer.

Solutions, however, occur when we see things in a new and fresh way — to allow our wisdom to come forth and take over. As ironic as it seems, we need to *stop thinking* about a problem in order to see the new solution! We need to use our "transmitter" instead of our "computer." As our minds clear of our concerns, answers will occur to us in ways we never thought possible. Wisdom becomes nothing more mystical than seeing the same old things in a nonhabitual manner — in a new and fresh way.

We have seen throughout this book that our thoughts grow with the attention we give them, and that the more we think about a given situation, the more real and formidable it will seem. Problems are certainly no exception!

Fred's Story

Fred was a consulting client of mine whose primary concern was money. He believed that despite his constant effort, there was never enough money to provide for his family. He had spent the last twenty years worrying, attempting to "think" of a good solution. He went over and over the same set of facts in his head, and every time he did so, he became despondent and frustrated.

Frustration is not the most productive state of mind — it is perhaps the least effective state we can be in. Thinking about something when we are frustrated doesn't work, because the problem is too close to us to allow a solution. Fred's well-intentioned obsession with money was merely creating more frustration, and no solutions.

As Fred began to see how his own thinking was working against him rather than for him, he stepped back, slowed down, and quieted his mind. As his confusion lessened, he found a more positive feeling state within himself and the answers to his problem. Fred realized that he had always been capable of solving the money question all along, once he simply stopped paying so much attention to it.

It turned out the "solution" lay in a hobby that Fred had been engaged in for many years. With a quieter mind and with broader perspective, he saw how he could turn that hobby into a business opportunity — and did so. Today he has the extra money he always felt he needed.

Virtually all of us have gone through a similar process attempting to solve problems that have come up in our lives. A friend of mine calls this process "the snowball effect." As we think about a problem, it grows in our minds. As it grows, we think the problem has gotten worse because we now see it in more detail and "more clearly." Because we see more of the problem than we did before, it grows bigger, so we tell our friends and family about it. Pretty soon they're agreeing with us. Now we *really* have a problem!

Einstein once said, "The solution to a problem will never come about from the same level of understanding that created the problem in the first place." I believe what he meant is that we need to step back from the problem in order to see a solution. Stepping back is another way of saying, "stop focusing on it."

You have probably had the experience of thinking about something obsessively, in an honest attempt to find an answer. You thought about it, and thought about it, and finally you gave up and looked out the window and noticed the beautiful scenery or soaked in a bathtub to relax. At that very moment, the answer came to you. "That's it!" you exulted, "That's the answer I have been waiting for." Unfortunately, as I mentioned at the beginning of this book, you might mistakenly have assumed that it was all the obsessive thought that finally created the answer. It was not! The answer came to you through your own source of wisdom — a place beyond your thinking — from a momentary feeling of contentment and relaxation. You already knew the facts and had all the data you needed. What you finally did was clear the way for an answer to surface. You got out of your own way!

This process of not thinking so much about problems works beautifully in marriage or relationship situations. I have seen many couples who have been bickering and fighting for years over the same things. Individually, each person would confess to spending an enormous amount of their waking day thinking about how bad their marriage was. Little did they know that their attention to these thoughts made it impossible to have a good marriage: their major focus was on how bad the marriage was. These couples had spent many years perfecting the art of a bad marriage in their heads — they had gone over and over the same things in an attempt to "straighten each other out."

Almost without exception, people who are exposed to an understanding of the process of thought are able to see this dynamic and almost *instantly* improve their relationships. Their new understanding has less to do with pretending that things don't bother them than with understanding why things had bothered them in the first place. It has to do with creating common-sense solutions to everyday issues.

Our Problems Become
a Major Source of Conversation

Focusing on our problems is just a bad habit. We become so accustomed to thinking about "what's wrong" that our problems become a major source of conversation with others. Focusing on something that bothers us, whatever it is, will not make us feel better. If we feel that someone has mistreated us in some way, talking about it won't help. If we had a "bad day" at work or at home, thinking about it won't help. If circumstances seem hopeless, dwelling on them won't help. What *will* help is to increase the positive feeling state in ourselves by not focusing on the problems, not giving them the energy and attention they need to grow in our minds, which only makes them seem worse. We do this not to avoid facing the problems but to *make room* for solutions to grow.

Your "Back Burner" Gives You Your Answer

Sometimes, solving a problem means that we have a question on our mind that we need an answer to. Perhaps we need to make an important decision or decide between two seemingly equal choices. Use your "back burner" to help you.

Each of us has access to a "back burner," a quiet place in the back of the mind where answers and solutions can grow and develop — without the interference of excess thought.

Using your back burner is quite simple. You tell yourself that you need an answer to a certain question within a given time frame. Then, rather than racking your brain for the answer, you deliberately forget about it! Automatically, like magic, an answer will soon pop into your head. You may be quite surprised and delighted when the answer you get is much better than the answer you would have come up with from struggling with the question. Give this process a try — you'll be so glad you did!

Use this technique when you're trying to decide where to go on vacation. Absorb the facts, including the costs, then tell yourself you will make a decision within the day. At that point, forget about your vacation and all the information. Your back burner will process the data and very shortly your answer will appear.

The "Time Factor" in Healing Painful Events

If we consider the way most people get over problems, by far the most popular way seems to be the "passage of time." We have been taught to believe that "time heals all wounds." And while this may be partially true, it's important to understand the true nature of the passage of time. Once we do, we can drastically reduce the time between experiencing painful events and getting over them.

If ten people experienced an identical situation, each of them would forget their trauma within a different time frame. Suppose that these ten people were held up in a bank, and none of them was robbed, but each was held at gunpoint while the criminals stole money from the bank's vault.

Some of the ten people (probably very few) would shake off the unfortunate incident as bad luck, and after consulting with the police, would go back to their daily routine. They would be grateful they were unharmed. Others would continue to feel frightened for days or even weeks and need to take time off from work and other daily commitments. There would be others who simply couldn't forget the incident and would believe it to be the cause of their continued unsettled feeling. They might take years (if ever) to get back to normal. They would talk about it, focus on it, think about it, keep themselves up at night, or even seek out help from a mental health professional. These people would tell you that "it takes a long time to get over something this traumatic."

Why is it that some people are able to shake off unfortunate incidents, while others dwell on them and use them as excuses to inhibit and immobilize their lives? The simple answer to this question is that some people understand thought and memory better than others. Some people understand that when we think about something, whether it be in the past or the future, our thought will bring whatever it is we are thinking about to life as if it were happening right now. The more detail and focus we put on it, the more real it will seem.

The passage of time has no relevance in helping us to get over something, other than to encourage us to forget it. There is no preset amount of time that will allow us to forget anything. Once we understand the dynamics of thought, we can see that all memory is only memory, whether something happened eight years ago or eight minutes ago. If the passage of time was the determining factor, everyone would get over things within the same time period. But we know this doesn't happen.

This understanding has enormous practical implications. Whereas once we might have set up an artificial time frame to recover from a situation, we can now see that it's up to us to determine how long or short a time it will take. For example, if we had a fight with someone, there is no preset time frame in which we can expect to get over it and forgive. If it usually takes us a week to get over an argument, this means that one week from the fight we stop thinking about it. Since the entire incident is over and now only goes on in our head, if we want to, we can stop paying attention to our thinking about the fight *ten minutes* after it's over. Once we have experienced how nice it is to live in a positive state of mind, hanging on to negative thoughts becomes less and less attractive.

What about our problems as they relate to our past? If old problems or hurts are now true only in our memory, why do they have to continue to immobilize us in the present? They don't! Anything we went through — whether it was growing up with demanding parents, a painful divorce, financial difficulty, childhood abuse, or anything else — does not *have to* prevent us from enjoying our life now, that is, if we understand that it is our memory that is carrying these events through time, nothing else. If we can learn to stop frightening ourselves with our own thoughts, we are on our way to a happier life irrespective of what we had to go through. It is our ability to forget our problems, through an understanding of the process of thought, rather than the passage of time, that frees us from the circumstances of our past.

If, in order to get over things, we depend solely on the passage of time and not on our own free will and ability to think (or not think), we will have set up a "cause-and-effect" relationship. If we believe that it takes a predetermined amount of time to recover from an event, this will ensure our unhappiness, because situations will continue to happen that are beyond our control. When we set up arbitrary time frames, we validate the belief that thought is something to fear and that we are victims of our past and what we think about. However, this need not be true.

There is an important distinction between understanding thought and denying it. Understanding our ability to think allows us to see that thought, in and of itself, is harmless. The fact that something comes to our mind does not necessarily make it worthy of our concern. Denial, on the other hand, suggests a sort of pretending that we are not thinking about something, or that a problem doesn't bother us. The two are not related. If we understand the process of thought, we are free of its adverse effects on us. But if we deny that we are thinking about something or that something is bothering us, we will still feel the effects of the thoughts we are denying. There is no escaping thought — there is only understanding.

Once again we can see the importance of a happy feeling — that feeling of peace and contentment that comes from a quiet mind. In that more positive feeling state, solving problems isn't nearly as difficult as it used to be.

CHAPTER NINE

HAPPINESS

People are just about as happy
as they make up their minds to be.

— Abraham Lincoln

HAPPINESS IS A STATE OF MIND, not a set of circumstances. It is a serene feeling you can always experience and live in, not something you have to search very far for. In fact, you can never find happiness by "searching," because the moment you do, you imply that it is found outside yourself. Happiness isn't outside yourself. It is a feeling — the natural feeling of your innate healthy psychological functioning.

When you understand and learn to flow with your own psychological functioning, you can access that place inside yourself where serenity already exists. Then you can stop trying to be happy and simply *be* happy. Even when your circumstances are less than perfect, that contented feeling can still be accessed because the feeling comes from within you, not from outside.

If you don't understand your own psychological functioning, however, you won't be happy, no matter how wonderful your circumstances are. You will continue to pay attention to your negative thoughts, as you have in the past, and keep feeling the painful effects of your own thinking.

The principles laid out in this book point directly toward happiness. They give you an understanding of how to keep your mind in sync with a happy feeling, and warn you how easy it is for your mind to pull you away from this contented state, if you insist on following your negative trains of thought to create "thought attacks."

Happiness Lies in the Present Moment

Happiness is now. It is innate. It occurs when you allow your mind to rest, when you take your focus of attention off your concerns and problems and instead allow your mind to relax and to remain right here in this moment. I don't mean "relax" in the sense of laziness or apathy, but rather in the sense of letting your mind take in information — and then letting it flow back out without holding on to it for analysis. If you take in information and stimulus in this manner, you can maintain the nicer feeling state, being happy with the tasks at hand. Once you understand your own psychological functioning, you will know that this mind relaxation is not lazy, it is smart. Only in a nicer feeling state, not a state of irritation, can new answers to old problems arise. Happiness allows you to see information in new and creative ways and to make rational, productive decisions in a timely manner; it allows you to enjoy, rather than struggle with, the ebbs and flows of life, and it encourages your wisdom and common sense to surface.

Coming up with theories as to why you are (or behave in) a certain way, or delving into your past to uncover painful memories will not bring you happiness. It will take you away from happiness — far from the direction you wish to be headed. Excessive thinking about your past and your problems will convince you that you do, in fact, have good reasons to be upset and unhappy.

But you don't want to be unhappy. And your past is over. It is a harmless memory, carried through time, through your own thinking. It was real then, but it isn't now. You can learn from your past, but it is a mistake to continually go into your past or overanalyze life in a search for happiness. If this worked, you'd be happy already! How many times have you unsuccessfully tried to think your way to happiness?

Who would you rather be? Person A, whose past was painful, but who has come to an understanding of thought and its effects on him? Or Person B, whose early life was almost magical, yet who now focuses on those few elements of his past that were less than perfect, and who believes those thoughts to the point of letting them depress him? Person A, despite his painful past, is capable of living a fully functional and very happy life, while Person B is tormented, not by his life as it is right now, but by his own thoughts that he takes too seriously. Person B, despite an outwardly wonderful life, is bound for years of unhappiness, therapy, and tranquilizers.

If you think too much or talk to others about how someone "wronged you," you won't feel happy. If you constantly think about how much better your life will be once the kids grow up, or once you're married, you won't feel happy either. This doesn't mean that you can't or shouldn't think about these (or other) things. But if you obsess on these thoughts, you will sacrifice a most powerful sense of well-being — the inherent feeling of happiness you were born with and still have access to.

Happiness and Desire

Anticipation feels better than anxiety — but it's not happiness. Thinking about the future and setting goals is fine, but don't mistake it for the simple, uncomplicated, noncontingent feeling of happiness: the feeling of being grateful right now for no reason other than the fact that you are alive.

Sometimes you might feel a moment or two of happiness right after getting something you want. Contrary to popular opinion, however, this is not because your desire was fulfilled, but because you took your attention off what you didn't have. The moment you switch gears and return your focus of attention to something else you want or don't have, you will lose your sense of well-being and feel discontent. Your mind will again begin searching for something outside itself to gain satisfaction — perpetuating the cycle of unhappiness.

If obtaining a desire — any desire — could be the cause of a feeling of happiness, we would all be happy already. But remember the countless times you have received what you wanted, yet didn't remain happy. I am not speaking of avoiding goals or desires. Happiness must come first. Anything that develops out of this happiness is wonderful, but fulfilled desire alone does not create happiness.

Happiness versus Catharsis

Sometimes we make ill-fated attempts at happiness by talking about what's wrong, and the temporary relief that we subsequently feel is through catharsis. This happens at the conclusion of an event such as getting something off our chest or telling a friend off. Bang! Whatever was disturbing us is gone; our minds are clear for an instant and we feel better. But this process is like banging your head against a wall so that when you stop you'll feel better. There's no question that you'll feel better, but wouldn't it be easier not to bang your head?

The difference between happiness and catharsis is this: a happy person would disregard the negative thoughts about his friend because he knows that those thoughts will come and go depending on his mood. He always has the option of talking to his friend at a later date if his thoughts are valid, but the best solution now is to clear his mind and enjoy his friend. He wants to be happy, and he doesn't want to disturb the good feeling that exists in the friendship.

A person who relies on catharsis, however, wants to get

his thoughts off his chest as soon as possible. He's had some negative thoughts about his friend and feels it's important to "release them." To him, being honest with his feelings is very important. It doesn't matter what his mood level is — he's having negative thoughts about his friend and he must tell him now! He wants to get it over with — he wants to be "right."

"But I'm Just Being Honest with My Feelings."

Being honest with your feelings is a relative thing. Are you being honest in a low mood, after your own thoughts have upset you, or are you being honest from a place of happiness and wisdom? This distinction is very important because your life, and everything in it, will look drastically different depending on your level of well-being. I know many people (myself included) who were champions at thinking we were "being honest," only to find that honesty is a very relative characteristic. The very same things that torment us in an upset state of mind don't bother us at all in a higher, more pleasant, state of mind.

Until you understand this concept, you might feel the need to react to each negative thought that enters your mind — in the name of being honest. But you can stop reacting to negativity and wait for a nicer feeling to surface before acting upon your thoughts. If you can wait, you will find that many, if not all, of your negative thoughts will dissipate, and you will find yourself saying things to yourself like, "Silly me, he's not such a bad guy. What was I thinking about?" and so forth. You will also have far more clarity, wisdom, and common sense available to you to make decisions.

Don't Attach Conditions to Your Happiness

Happiness cannot occur when we place its source outside of ourselves. Once we assume that certain conditions must be met before we can feel happy, we are too late to experience it. Most of us do experience fleeting moments of happiness, but let them pass us by without due notice. We fail to recognize the feeling of happiness for what it is and inadvertently let it drift away with our thoughts. We do this because we are always looking to find happiness somewhere else.

Whenever you attach conditions to your happiness, you won't experience it. The same mental process that attaches your happiness to a specific outcome will repeat the process once that outcome is obtained. A woman who believes that getting married will make her happy, will then create new conditions to be met once the marriage is in place. She may then believe that children will be the answer — purchasing a home, a promotion, whatever. Once this trend is established, few people question their poor results. Why aren't we happy yet?

When you can recognize the feeling of happiness when it's there, you will realize that this feeling is what you have been looking for all along. *The feeling isn't leading somewhere else — it's the goal, not the means to a goal.* If the bride-to-be understands that her happiness comes first from within, she can make the decision to marry or not to marry from a place of wisdom, not from a place of lack. If she is already happy, the marriage will also be happy. If the couple then decides to have children, the children will grow up in a happy environment without the pressure of being someone's source of happiness. The same will be true throughout the life of any happy person. Happiness breeds a happy existence and a joyous way of looking at life.

You won't keep your contentment if it depends on a ritual or a technique: if you attach your happiness to doing something right, you will often find yourself disappointed. I've known many people who have said, "I'm doing everything right — how come I'm so miserable?" The reasons are always the same. If exercising is your "technique," what happens if you can't exercise? Even more important, exercise doesn't equate to happiness. If it did, all people who exercise would be happy all of the time — but they're not. This isn't to say that techniques are bad, and they can be useful for many different reasons. But techniques in themselves don't have the power to make you happy. Techniques can help you reach certain goals, but they don't create the feeling of happiness.

Happiness Is a Feeling, Not an Outcome

When you understand that happiness is nothing more than a feeling, you can help it to grow and maintain itself when you do feel it. When you place your attention on your feeling of happiness, you will notice that your mind is relatively clear — that your thinking is diffuse. If you are thinking at all, it's only on the task at hand, not on the outcome or on self-evaluation. It's not that you shouldn't think; in fact, in this nicer feeling state, you have complete access to your best thinking, your wisdom and common sense. In this nicer feeling state, your mind is disengaged — not overly focused on the content of your thinking.

In this state of mind (which is available to anyone at anytime) it is possible to maintain your happiness, even if things around you aren't to your personal liking. Happiness is a feeling, not an outcome; know what to look for and you will be able to stay in this feeling, rather than missing it and continuing to look elsewhere.

As you experience the feeling of happiness, don't think about it. If you do, it will leave you. If you understand the dynamics of your own mind, this won't be a problem. As you quietly recognize serenity in your life, it will stay with you for longer periods of time. And when you lose the feeling, it will come back more quickly. The key is to *understand* the dynamic, not to think about it, just notice the feeling without analyzing it. Thinking requires effort, however small. Happiness requires no effort at all. In fact, it's more of a letting go of unhappiness than it is a striving for happiness. "Letting go" is nothing more than taking your attention off whatever it is you are thinking about — not forcefully but easily.

"Happiness comes from within" is a cliché, but it is true. Happiness is the way, the only answer you need. When you understand your own mental process, you naturally see and feel the beauty in life. When you're in your positive feeling state, what once seemed urgent and upsetting seems insignificant. And the simple beauty in life that you took for granted for so long — children playing in your neighborhood, a gentle breeze, people helping others — you now see with new, appreciative eyes. When happiness is your goal, you can experience it regardless of your surroundings. When you understand how to realize your own contentment, you will no longer choose to entertain thoughts that take you away from this wondrous goal.

Happiness is right now. Your life is not a dress rehearsal for some later date — it is right here, right now. The invisible quality of happiness we have all been looking for is right here in a feeling.

CHAPTER TEN

Habits and
ADDICTIONS

A habit is a thought that you have accepted as truth.

— Richard Carlson

I N AN EARLIER BOOK, *Everything I Eat Makes Me Thin*, I discussed how a specific habit (overeating) originates and develops into a problem. My intent here is more general. I hope that after reading this chapter, you will understand habits in a way that will help you, whatever your habits may be. I use the words "habit" and "addiction" interchangeably here to describe any behavior you engage in that, given a choice, you would rather not.

Because all habits originate in an identical manner, the specific habits you are working with are not important. What is important is to begin to see where habits come from and the most effective way to eliminate them as a source of distress in your life.

Happiness is a positive feeling that exists inside you, and in this book we have discussed how to remove the psychological blocks to this happiness. When you live in this positive state of mind, you have a sense of balance and ease. Whenever you lose this positive feeling, you knowingly or unknowingly attempt to get it back. The dynamics of healthy psychological functioning tell us that you get your positive feeling back by releasing the thoughts that are taking your good feelings away. When you don't understand the dynamics of your own mind, you innocently attempt to get your positive feeling back through outside sources — which can be the beginning of bad habits. Some popular substitutes for a contented state of mind are alcohol, drugs, cigarettes, food, exercise, gambling, sex, and work. A few of the more subtle forms include arguing, fighting, proving yourself, and approval seeking.

Realize Serenity in Your Life

Whether your addiction takes the form of approval seeking or alcohol, the first step to recovery is to realize serenity in your life. Serenity or contentment is the breeding ground for positive change. The opposite of serenity, insecurity, is the breeding ground for addictions. If you have serenity, eliminating bad habits is both possible and enjoyable, but without serenity, change is difficult, almost impossible. Thus, any attempt to cure an addiction without first acquiring a feeling of contentment is like bailing out a leaking boat. You can stay afloat, but only with absurdly hard and consistent work.

The inherent need to search for a positive feeling in our lives cannot be overstated. I believe it is the most important part of my life. Without a positive state of mind, I feel empty and alone — I have nothing. I will do anything it takes, even something harmful to myself or others, to fill up my emptiness. This emptiness is at the root of all addictions and habits, and just as the cause of all addictions is the same, so is the solution. My solution is to access my healthy psychological functioning — that nice feeling of contentment that tells me I already have what I want out of life.

Habits can always be traced back to your own thinking. If you think about something, food, for example, your thoughts will create a feeling inside you called an "urge." This compelling feeling creates in you the desire to satisfy that urge — in the case of food — by eating.

Take Your Attention Off Your Habits

Common sense will tell you that the more you think about something, the more those thoughts will grow in your mind and become real. Despite common sense, many addiction-recovery centers and addiction specialists would have you think of little else besides your addiction. They have you remind yourself — and others — of your problem many times a day. They counsel you to think and talk about what it's like to be an addict.

The reason these addiction specialists have us focus on our problem (habit) is to keep us from denying the fact that we do indeed have a problem. And while they are often successful in achieving this goal, the act of focusing on the problem or habit will make it grow in our minds and seem more formidable, more difficult to solve. So, while focus does keep us out of denial, we are also validating the severity and complexity of our habit, which confirms it will be difficult to overcome.

One common denominator exists in almost all people with a weight problem: food is constantly on their minds. Most weight loss programs are ultimately unsuccessful because they encourage participants to focus on food — what to eat, when to eat, how to eat, where to eat, and how much to eat.

In order to lose weight, you must take your attention off food. Food must be less on your mind — not more. The same is true with any habit. If you walk around all day thinking about cigarettes, it's going to be very difficult not to smoke. If you keep thinking about how much you dislike your spouse, it's going to be hard to feel love when you come home. Your energy always follows your attention. If your attention is directed toward food, that is where your energy will go.

There is an old saying: "Don't fuel the fire." If habits are your fire, then thinking is gasoline. The more gasoline you pour in the fire, the larger it becomes. So too with habits — the more you think about them, the seemingly bigger they become.

It is not my intention or my place to speak disparagingly

about any recovery center or form of treatment. There are many good centers and programs throughout the world helping millions of people with all types of addictions. But I would add something to the programs. The dimension of recovery that is necessary to be free of a negative habit is the part that includes education about mental health, contentment, and positive feelings, as well as about the patterns of addiction.

There is a way to become free of your habits *without denying* that you have them. This comes about by understanding how thought feeds on itself and becomes a reality in your mind and, conversely, through understanding how to achieve a nicer, more peaceful state of mind on a regular basis.

Recovery centers and addiction specialists are correct to assert that you need resolve to break a habit, particularly a severe one. But this resolve should not be reflected on moment to moment, day in and day out. Rather it is a deep yet soft commitment to yourself to stop a destructive force in your life. It is an inner knowing that *now* is the time that you need to stop. Once you have made this personal resolve, you are no longer in denial, but are on the road to freedom. Continuing to focus obsessively on your habit at this point serves to hurt rather than help you.

Happiness, Resolve, and Understanding

The ingredients needed to break any habit are *happiness, resolve, and understanding*. Happiness is the breeding ground that makes recovery possible, resolve is the inner commitment that points to your goal, and understanding is the vehicle to take you there.

Understanding your own psychological functioning allows you to think about something, even a habit that has become a problem, without taking your thoughts so seriously as to frighten yourself. When you are able to witness your thoughts and not become immersed in them, you can be more graceful in your lower moods and also be wary of yourself in these low states. Take advantage of your negative feelings by using them as warning signals. They alert you that you are thinking in a dysfunctional manner and could be headed toward unhappiness or destructive habits. You will have the wisdom to see your bad habits as nothing more than negative thoughts that you have come to accept as truth.

You have learned throughout this book about the truly harmless nature of your thoughts: thinking is a gift, a wonderful ability that you have, but you don't need to take this function or the content of your thoughts too seriously. For habits to become harmless, they too must be seen as nothing more than thoughts that you are unnecessarily accepting as reality. You never need to be frightened by your own thoughts.

I have now come full circle back to my initial discussion of thought. Now that you understand the potentially harmless and arbitrary nature of thought — the fact that it is something we are doing all the time — you don't need to be victimized by it. It is rather a question of determining your relationship to your own thinking. Do you see your thinking as an ability you have to bring meaning to your life, or do you see it as a "reality" that must be feared and responded to? Your answer to this question will determine your effectiveness in eliminating habits as a destructive force in your life. The greater your level of understanding, the easier it will get.

Your mastery of this understanding will allow you to remove the psychological blocks that prevent you from enjoying your most natural state — that of contentment.

CHAPTER ELEVEN

A Checklist for
YOUR LIFE

IF YOU ARE EXPERIENCING anything other than contentment that comes from self-understanding, it may be useful to ask yourself the following questions.

1. *Is my life really all that bad right now, or am I simply in a low mood?*

Our mood is the source of our experience, not the effect of it. If we are feeling poorly, our life will seem worse than it really is. If we are feeling low, the best thing to do is slow our thinking down, take our mind off whatever it is on, wait for the mood to pass, and look for a nicer feeling. Life and everything in it will appear much better soon!

2. Am I following the road toward unhappiness in an attempt to find happiness?

If I wanted to make a trip from San Francisco to New York, I would head due east, but if I went south instead, I would find Los Angeles — not where I meant to go. The same principle applies to finding a feeling of contentment. If you often find yourself expressing or thinking negatively, this is not the road to happiness. Any thoughts that take us away from a positive feeling are not worth having or defending. If you want to be happy, follow your happy feelings, not your unhappy ones.

3. Am I putting my opinions above my positive feelings?

Let us ask ourselves the question: "Do I want to be right, or do I want to be happy?" When we take our opinions so seriously that they bring us discontented feelings, they are not worth defending. It is possible to maintain our valid, strong beliefs in a positive feeling state, and these positions will be more seriously respected by others when we demonstrate a positive state of mind.

4. Am I reacting to someone else's low mood?

It's easy to forget that we all have mood swings. If we remember that everyone, even the nicest person, has moods, we won't take their attacks on us personally — they are not directed at us. Moods are a fact of life. Everyone, those we work with and are close to, will experience the ups and downs of moods. In low moods, people will say and do things that they wouldn't even dream of in higher states of mind. This doesn't mean we must accept abuse from people, but that we make allowances in our minds and hearts for the psychological fact of moods. When we accept the inevitability of moods, we will cease to take them so personally.

5. *Am I playing out a war in my own head?*

Most arguments take place in our minds, either before or after the actual event. If the thoughts that are creating a discontented feeling enter our heads, they are merely harmless thoughts — not reality. If we have a conflict, its resolution will come more easily when we are at a higher feeling level. We are the producers of our own thoughts. Recognizing that we are doing the thinking can end the mental war, and we can then turn away from the war and toward a nicer feeling.

6. *Am I struggling with a problem?*

Thoughts grow with attention. Our energy will go where our attention is. If we continually struggle with a problem, we block our channel of wisdom and common sense. To effectively solve a current problem, we need to distance ourselves from it. Whenever anything is too close to us, it is difficult to see with clear eyes. As we let go of the problem, the answers that seemed elusive will present themselves.

7. *Is my tolerance for stress too high?*

The level of stress in our lives will always be exactly the same as our current tolerance level. There is a tendency, when we feel stressed to put our foot to the floor, roll up our sleeves, and get to work. Despite the urgency we feel, a reduction in stress will never be the result. When we feel stressed, it's time to ease up, take a break, stop thinking so much, clear our minds. When we do so, we will feel better and rebound quickly. To live a life of reduced stress, the goal is to lower our tolerance to stress. In time, we will be able to catch stress early on and eliminate it before it can overwhelm us.

8. *Am I thinking about myself too much?*

Evaluating yourself or your performance too much will serve to lower your spirits. Thinking too much about how you're doing takes you away from your natural sense of self-esteem and happiness. We need only to watch small children to remember that we are all naturally proud of our efforts. Through self-doubt we lose our sense of self-worth. Live each moment to its fullest — enjoy each precious hour of life that you are given. If we all approach our lives in this manner, the details, our accomplishments and responsibilities, will work themselves out — they really will. And what's more, we'll enjoy ourselves in the process.

9. *Am I taking my past with me?*

The past is a memory that we carry through our own thinking. Whether something happened twenty years ago or twenty minutes ago, what's past is not relevant to our ability to enjoy our lives now, at this moment. As our understanding of the dynamics of thought deepens, we will be freed of the adverse effects of our unhappy pasts.

10. Am I postponing my life?

It's been said that "Life is what happens to you while you're busy making other plans." Whenever we defer happiness, we fail to recognize that happiness is a feeling we already have, that we can access at will. It is not contingent on outcomes. If you find yourself saying things like, "I'll be happy when," you are missing out. Happiness happens whenever you tap into your own naturally healthy psychological functioning. You can be happy right here, right now, if you choose to do so.

About the
AUTHOR

Richard Carlson, PhD, is considered one of the foremost experts on happiness in the United States. He is a nationally acclaimed speaker who has spoken to audiences of thousands. His books, with more than twenty-six million copies in print, include the bestselling *Don't Sweat the Small Stuff* series and *Don't Worry, Make Money*. He is the coeditor, with Benjamin Shield, PhD, of *Handbook for the Soul, Handbook for the Heart,* and *For the Love of God: Handbook for the Spirit*. He is a popular talk show guest, having appeared on hundreds of radio and television shows, including *Good Morning America, The Today Show,* and *Oprah*.